rebuilt and RESTORED

God's Wonderful Work of Renewal
LESSONS FROM THE BOOK OF NEHEMIAH

Authors

Ali Shaw • Alyssa Howard • Ayoka Billions

Jennifer McLucas • Karen Bozeman • Kat Lee • Kelly LaFram

Hellomornings.org

REBUILT AND RESTORED

© 2017 HelloMornings

ALL RIGHTS RESERVED

No part of this book may be reproduced in any form or by any electronic or mechanical means, including information storage and retrieval systems, without written permission from the author, except in the case of a reviewer, who may quote brief passages embodied in critical articles or in a review.

TABLE OF CONTENTS

THE NEW Hellomornings BIBLE STUDY METHOD V

SHARE THE STUDY VII
   The Big Bible Study Idea List . . . . *viii*
   Read And Write . . . . *viii*
   Respond . . . . *ix*
   Research . . . . *x*
   Ready To Dive In? . . . . *xi*

INTRODUCTION 2

WEEK ONE 4
   Week 1, Day 1: 2 KINGS 24:8-17 . . . . *4*
   Week 1, Day 2: 2 Kings 24:18–25:2 . . . . *6*
   Week 1, Day 3: 2 Kings 25:8-12, 2 Kings 17:7 and 19-20 . . . . *8*
   Week 1, Day 4: Nehemiah 1:1-3 . . . . *10*
   Week 1, Day 5: Nehemiah 1:4-11 . . . . *12*

WEEK TWO 14
   Week 2, Day 1: Nehemiah 2:1-5 . . . . *14*
   Week 2, Day 2: Nehemiah 2:6-8 . . . . *16*
   Week 2, Day 3: Nehemiah 2:9-10 . . . . *18*
   Week 2, Day 4: Nehemiah 2:11-16 . . . . *20*
   Week 2, Day 5: Nehemiah 2:17-20 . . . . *22*

WEEK THREE 24
   Week 3, Day 1: 1 Nehemiah 3:1, 4:1-5 . . . . *24*
   Week 3, Day 2: Nehemiah 4:6-9 . . . . *26*
   Week 3, Day 3: Nehemiah 4:10-14 . . . . *28*
   Week 3, Day 4: Nehemiah 4:15-23 . . . . *30*
   Week 3, Day 5: Nehemiah 5:1, 6-11 . . . . *32*

WEEK FOUR 34
   Week 4, Day 1: Nehemiah 6:1-9 . . . . *34*
   Week 4, Day 2: Nehemiah 6:10-14 . . . . *36*
   Week 4, Day 3: Nehemiah 6:15-19 . . . . *38*
   Week 4, Day 4: Nehemiah 7:1-4 . . . . *40*
   Week 4, Day 5: Nehemiah 7:5-7, 66, 73 . . . . *42*

WEEK FIVE . . . . **.44**
    Week 5, Day 1: Nehemiah 8:1-12 . . . . *44*
    Week 5, Day 2: Nehemiah 8:13-18 . . . . *46*
    Week 5, Day 3: Nehemiah 9:1-5 . . . . *48*
    Week 5, Day 4: Nehemiah 9:6-8, 22-23, 26, 30-31 . . . . *50*
    Week 5, Day 5: Nehemiah 9:32-37 . . . . *52*

WEEK SIX . . . . **.54**
    Week 6, Day 1: Nehemiah 12:27-30, 40-43 . . . . *54*
    Week 6, Day 2: Nehemiah 12:44-47 . . . . *56*
    Week 6, Day 3: Nehemiah 13:1-14 . . . . *58*
    Week 6, Day 4: Nehemiah 13:15-22 . . . . *60*
    Week 6, Day 5: Nehemiah 13:23-31 . . . . *62*

CONCLUSION . . . . **.64**

ABOUT THE AUTHORS . . . . **.65**

THE NEW Hellomornings BIBLE STUDY METHOD

We (The HelloMornings Team) are SO excited to share this new Bible study method with you!

The heart behind the method is "For Every Woman in Every Season." Whether you have 5 minutes or 50 minutes every morning, the HelloMornings study method can adapt to your schedule. We designed it so that a new believer won't feel overwhelmed and a seasoned Bible study student can dive deep into each passage.

We had three main goals in creating this method:

1. TO BUILD YOUR HABIT

Because building a daily God time habit is at the core of HelloMornings, we want to make sure you never feel overwhelmed with each day's study. If you only have 5 minutes, you can read the passage, write the verse and respond in a written prayer. If you have more time, you can dig deeper with one, two or all of the study "action steps." And if you want to go even deeper (or stretch the study out to a Saturday or Sunday) we are including group of study ideas in the front of the ebook so you'll always have a treasure trove of options to choose from.

2. TO BUILD YOUR GROUP

Our second goal was to create a method that encourages group interaction. Groups are integral to what we do here at HelloMornings. They are a way to build community, stay accountable to growth and learn from different perspectives.

But it's hard to find a group where everyone is at the same level of studying Scripture. That means with most Bible studies, some group members feel overwhelmed while others feel bored. Our goal is to bridge that gap and create content that not only fits any schedule, but also fits any level of study.

The beauty of this is that someone in your group who is brand new to the faith can daily dive into the same scriptures as a group leader who has been studying for decades. And the way we have formatted the content allows for each to learn and share in whatever way God is leading them so everyone can feel they have something to contribute, if they choose.

3. TO BUILD YOUR ROUTINE

In order to be the "hands and feet of Jesus," we need to:

1. Know Him - (God)
2. Understand His purpose for our lives - (Plan)
3. Follow His leading - (Move)

These are the core habits of HelloMornings.

God. Plan. Move.

Time with God is essential. And we believe that God has a purpose for each one of our lives. We also believe that He even has a purpose for each of our days. There are people He may want you to encourage today or ways He wants you to take action.

That is why we Plan. We want our daily planning to be done with His purposes in mind. Each daily worksheet has space for just a few of the most important tasks. Prayerfully planning is more powerful than any fancy productivity system because only God knows our heart, our purpose and our circumstances.

Finally, it's time to Move. This doesn't need to be a 3-mile run or a 25-minute workout. We simply want to be "fit for our calling" - i.e. have the energy to walk out the plan toward our purpose. If God has things He'd like us to do today, it's our responsibility to have the energy to do them. He does not give us more than we can handle.

For some, this might be simply drinking a morning glass of water. For others, it might be a short workout and for others it might be a healthy breakfast. The goal is just to do what we can to have the energy to respond to whatever God is calling us to each day. Kind of like an athlete makes sure to eat a good breakfast before a game so she has the energy to play well.

God. Plan. Move.

It doesn't need to take a long time. It could be as simple as a 5-minute routine of reading the daily passage, jotting down a few tasks and drinking a glass of water. Or it could be longer and more customized to your life.

Ultimately, we just want to start each day with the One who gave us all our days. And we want to plan our lives with the One who gives us our lives. And we want to Move wherever He may lead.

To a life well lived for the good of others and the glory of God,

The HelloMornings Team

SHARE THE STUDY

Will you consider helping us spread the word?

If you're in a HelloMornings group, invite all your group members to upgrade from the basic reading plan to this full study. It is well worth the price of a latte to study scripture deeply for 6 weeks and build a solid morning routine.

If you don't have a HelloMornings group, gather some friends together, send them to *HelloMornings.org/shop* to grab a copy of the study and spend the next 6 weeks journeying together! It's so much more fun and impactful when we learn and grow in community.

WAYS TO HELP OTHERS:

Use the hashtag *#HelloMornings* on Twitter or Instagram.

Share what you're learning on Facebook and link to *HelloMornings.org*

Tell your friends! Text, email or invite them to join you the next time you see them.

GET ALL THE RESOURCES:

We want to equip you to build a brilliant, God centered morning routine that leaves you feeling refueled and ready for action each day.

If you're not already on our email list, visit *HelloMornings.org* to download our free resources and receive our inspiring and idea-filled newsletter.

THE BIG BIBLE STUDY IDEA LIST

Each day of a HelloMornings study is filled with passages to read, a verse to write and plenty of action steps to take. But if you're ready to dive even deeper or you want to stretch our 5 day a week studies into 7 days, this list is the perfect way for you to add "tools" to your Bible study tool belt.

If you finish the study for the day and have more time, simply refer back to this "Big Bible Study Idea List" to select a few ways to dive even deeper into the passage you've been reading.

The best thing about this list is that it can be used on ANY section of scripture. So, if you want to do a study on 1 Corinthians 13 or look up all the verses on Faith, just use this list to build your own Bible study!

We want to equip you to study the Bible deeply regardless of whether you have a Bible study guide you're going through at the time or not. Try out each of these "tools" and add them to your Bible study "tool belt!"

READ AND WRITE

Ways to study scripture and dig deep into one passage.

READ
Simply read the passage. You can read it in your head, read out loud, read thoughtfully and slow, read in another translation.

WRITE
Honestly, this is my favorite way to start each morning. I *love* writing out scripture. There's something about the process of handwriting that both wakes me up and allows me to really marinate in the passage. It's also incredibly meaningful to have notebooks filled with handwritten scripture.

IDENTIFY KEY VERSES
In the passage you're reading, which verse holds the nugget of wisdom. Which verses explain the transformation of the main characters. Which verses speak most deeply to you in the season you're in right now?

HIGHLIGHT, UNDERLINE, BRACKET, CIRCLE, JOT
In this digital age, there is something therapeutic about words on a paper page and a pack of highlighters or colored pencils. I always loved looking at my grandmothers Bible filled with highlights, underlines, notes and circles.

Take time to circle commands, underline truths or highlight key verses in your favorite shade of pink. Bible study can be fun and colorful!

OBSERVE
Let your inner Nancy Drew loose. Uncover the 5 W's of the passage. Who, What, When, Where, Why and (don't forget) How. It's amazing how much we can learn from just naming the different elements of a passage or story.

ILLUSTRATE
In the margins of your Bible, or on a HelloMornings worksheet, get creative! Design word art focusing on a key point. Sketch the setting, characters or theme.

OUTLINE
Feeling more cerebral than creative? Outline the story or teaching. Highlight the main points and the sub-points to develop a greater understanding of where the author was coming from and what he was trying to communicate.

PERSONAL PARAPHRASE
Sometimes we learn best by teaching. Imagine you had to share the heart of the passage with a group of friends or a class of children, how would you paraphrase it? Or paraphrase it by incorporating your story into it and the things God has done in your life. You could even paraphrase it by simply incorporating your name in everywhere it has a generic pronoun.

QUESTIONS
Got questions? Just write them down. You can answer them later. Don't let your questions keep you from getting through the passage. Imagine you could interview the author, what would you ask?

RESPOND

A great way to dig deeper into scripture is to as a few simple questions. You can think about the answers as you read or you can write down your responses on the HelloMornings worksheet or in your own journal.

The Bible truly comes alive when we consider and pray about how God wants us to apply it to our own lives.

QUESTIONS TO CONSIDER:
- What does this say about God?
- What does this say about the church?
- What does this say about me?

- What truths are in this passage?
- Does this passage lead me to confess anything in prayer?
- What should I pray?
- What actions should I take?
- How can today be different because of this passage?
- What are some journaling questions?
- What is the lesson from this passage?
- Which key verse should I memorize this week?

RESEARCH

There is so much to be learned on every page of scripture. But sometimes we can take our study to a new level when we start flipping the pages and learning the "story behind the story."

Here are a few things you can research about the passage you are studying.

AUTHOR
Who wrote this passage? What do we know about him and how he fits into the story of the Bible? What were his circumstances? Why did he write it? Who was he writing to? Where was he when he wrote it? What had God done in his life to compel him to write this passage?

BACKGROUND
What was the background of the passage? What story or theme was introduced in previous verses or chapters of the book?

AUDIENCE
Who was the audience that the author was writing to? Why was it written to them? How do you think they responded to it? How would you have responded?

CONTEXT: CULTURAL, HISTORICAL, GRAMMATICAL
What was happening in history at the time the passage was written? What was the culture in which it was written like? How did the culture or the historical circumstances influence the author? Are there any grammatical rhythms or clues identifying or strengthening the authors meaning or ultimate intent?

CROSS REFERENCE
If you have a Bible with cross references (or using an online resource), look up all the verses associated with the passage. What can you learn from them and how do they influence the text?

COMMENTARIES

Read the commentary in your Bible, commentary books or at a trusted online source to gain even more insight into the passage.

TRANSLATIONS

Read the passage in multiple translations. How do they differ? How are they the same? What new truths can you glean from the variety of perspectives?

MAPS

Are there any maps in your Bible or online related to the passage you're studying? Follow the journey of the main characters. Look up modern day pictures of the locations. Research how long their journeys may have taken or any obstacles they may have encountered in their travels (culturally or geographically).

WORD STUDY (ORIGINAL LANGUAGE)

Brush up on your Greek and Hebrew and study the passage in the original language using an interlinear Bible.

READY TO DIVE IN?

Feel free to refer back to this list at any point, but now it's time to dive into the new HelloMornings study.

Here we go...

Cheering you on,

Kat Lee and the *HelloMornings.org* Team

FREE AUDIO VERSION

Email your Amazon receipt to us and get the audio version of this study for free!

Audios@hellomornings.org

rebuilt and RESTORED

God's Wonderful Work of Renewal

LESSONS FROM THE BOOK OF NEHEMIAH

INTRODUCTION

IN MODERN TIMES, WE LIVE UNDER THE RULE OF GRACE brought about by our precious Savior, Jesus Christ. Aren't you thankful for that? The Jews living in Old Testament times weren't offered this magnificent experience. Instead, the Law was in place in order to hold God's people to a high standard of spiritual purity. Since our God is righteous, sin must be dealt with. Thankfully, our sin is washed away by the blood of Christ. However, the sin of the Jews was made evident by their rebellion against God's law, dealt with by God's judgment and discipline, and atoned for by sacrifices. The people of the nation of Israel were forced to leave their country and home following a Babylonian invasion and defeat by King Nebuchadnezzar during the 6th century B.C. They were subsequently forced to live in exile for 70 years. This was God's act of judgment on His people for their repeated acts of idolatry (see 2 Kings 17). God had warned them as early as Moses' time to continue faithfully obeying God or suffer the consequences (see Deuteronomy 28:45-52), but they were stiff-necked and rebellious. It took an exile to a foreign land for the Jews to repent of their idolatry. But during this Babylonian exile, the Jewish people maintained many aspects of their national culture and lived out a rededicated, repentant worship. (The Book of Esther gives us insight into how the Jews lived in the Persian Empire after Persia had conquered Babylon.)

But Babylon was not home. The Israelites longed for the day when they could return to their own land. The prophet Ezekiel was one of several prophets who urged the people to repent of their sins and helped maintain the hope of return to the land that had been promised to Abraham many centuries before.

Ezra (whose name means "helper") and Nehemiah (whose name means "comfort" or "comforted by God") were used by God to illustrate a helpful, comforting love to a wayward people in need of a restored relationship with Him. Their love for their people and homeland foreshadowed Christ's love for the world. Though likely written by their individual namesakes, the Books of Ezra and Nehemiah were originally published as one scroll by the Hebrews and weren't commonly published separately until the Latin Vulgate was written. Together, these books chronicle the story of God's people returning to their beloved home, the urgent need to repair the Temple and the following task of repairing Jerusalem's wall and gates. (For more insight into this period, you can look into the prophets Zechariah and Haggai who lived during this period of Jewish history.)

Nehemiah tells us of a God who performs wonderful works of renewal! Yes, Nehemiah explains that our God used his obedience and the obedience of the Jewish nation to rebuild the wall and gates of Jerusalem and restore the relationship between God and His beloved people. Yes, our Lord works renewal, both in the physical world around us and within our hearts. He desires a healthy, Father-child relationship with us and pursues us intently.

Pray with us?

Lord, open our eyes to see your marvelous hand in the rebuilding and restoring of the city walls and gates Nehemiah describes. Also, Lord, reveal any places inside of us that you need to rebuild and restore. Help us to walk in obedience and surrender ourselves completely to you! Forgive us for any waywardness or stubbornness. Heal our hearts and build us up into the daughters of God that you desire us to be…all for your names' sake and your glory, Amen.

Ali and Ayoka

WEEK ONE
by Ali Shaw

WEEK 1, DAY 1: 2 KINGS 24:8-17

I'VE ALWAYS LOVED HISTORY. Learning from those who've gone before us is invaluable. So bear with me, friends, and let's dive into a super quick history lesson! This review will help us understand the book Nehemiah better and we can also learn from the godly and be warned by the wicked.

Let's start with Moses. Remember how God used Moses to lead the Israelites back to the land He'd originally promised Abraham? Well, after that, judges ruled until Israel demanded a person-king, rather than have God as king. First came King Saul. After his disobedience (1 Samuel 13:11-15) God promised the Kingdom to David and that David's throne would be established forever. (See 2 Samuel 7:12-16)

This promise was fulfilled in two ways. First, Jesus was a physical descendant of David (see Matthew 1 and Luke 3) and, as we know, He reigns forever. Second, David's line continued to rule when his son, Solomon, gained the throne. (God kept His Word; while there were kings ruling Judah, each one descended from David.) But things changed under Solomon's son, Rehoboam. The kingdom was split in two parts, Israel and Judah. And for a long time, Judah remained faithful to God while Israel strayed.

Today, we've read about King Jehoiachin of Judah. In verse nine, we are told that Jehoiachin did evil like his father Jehoiakim (see 2 Kings 23:34). Interestingly, Jehoiakim's father, Josiah, had been a good king who purposed to follow God. (Sadly, our children don't always follow our lead.) But in previous generations, evil influences had entered the kingdom of Judah through the arranged marriage of evil Queen Jezebel's daughter of Israel to King Jehoram of Judah. After this marriage, many of the kings of Judah chose not to follow God. And this evil certainly left its mark on Jehoiachin.

Oh, what a responsibility we have in deciding whom we'll serve! (Joshua 24:15) Will we serve Jesus, the fulfilled promise of God and King who reigns forever? Or will we walk after our flesh? Like the kings we've discussed today, the choice is ours and the consequences are great! The ability to influence future generations by our spiritual legacy is in our hands. We may not know for sure what our descendants will choose (remember King Josiah's sons?), but we can definitely pray for our future generations and live worshipful lives with devoted hearts. Our faithful, promise-keeping God is able to use our legacy in His glorious work of rebuilding and renewal!

— **KEY VERSE** —

And he did what was evil in the sight of the LORD, according to all that his father had done. (2 Kings 24:9)

Hello mornings
God. Plan. Move.

GOD TIME

READ : 2 Kings 24:8-17
WRITE : 2 Kings 24:9

REFLECT :
- This passage is depressing but helps us gain understanding. List all that Nebuchadnezzar and his army did.
- To keep names straight, make a little family tree starting with Josiah. We'll add to this later.
- This was the second invasion of Jerusalem. Read 2 Kings 24:1-4 to learn about the first.
- What is God teaching you through this passage?
- What does today's passage lead you to pray? Ask Him to help you leave a worshipful legacy.

RESPOND :

PLAN TIME

THINGS TO DO (3-5 MAX) :

KEY EVENTS TODAY :

MOVE TIME

MORNING WATER ☐

B : _____
L : _____
D : _____

SNACK :

SIMPLE WORKOUT ☐

WEEK 1, DAY 2: 2 KINGS 24:18–25:2

MANY YEARS AGO, OUR FAMILY TOOK A TRIP TO ITALY and had the strangest thing happen! After a day out, we traveled to our hotel and the busy autostrade began to look deserted. It was dark, so we slowed down considerably because of the peculiarity of it all. Suddenly, the three-laned, paved highway in front of us ended *abruptly*. When we realized our path led us nowhere, we turned around and took another route.

Yesterday we talked about Jehoiakim and Jehoiachin. Today, we're introduced to King Zedekiah (originally named Mattaniah). History gets a little confusing here because instead of sons taking the throne from their fathers, we have uncles and brothers reigning. Remember good King Josiah who followed God? Well, he had three sons that reigned over Judah. First was Jehoahaz, then Jehoiakim, and after Jehoiachin's reign, Josiah's son Zedekiah was placed on the throne by Nebuchadnezzar as a "puppet king." He would have the appearance of ruling, but really, Nebuchadnezzar would have the ultimate authority. (Actually, God had the ultimate authority, and a descendant of David was even placed on the throne.)

Zedekiah could have easily looked at the legacy of his forefathers and brothers to know what spiritual paths in life were the ones to follow. But he didn't. Instead, he foolishly followed His wicked ancestors and discarded the good legacy of his father, Josiah. He thought he could do things his way and rely on his own strength in fighting against Nebuchadnezzar's imposing reign over the people of Judah. He didn't foresee God's righteous anger and judgment.

King Zedekiah reached out to Egypt for help when he decided to rebel against Babylon. Interestingly, Egypt is often used in the Bible as a symbol of sin and opposition to God. Whatever the symbolism here, it is obvious that wicked Zedekiah didn't go to God for wisdom and help; he sought chariots and warriors instead. If he'd have looked into things further, he might have realized God's plan to enact judgement and righteousness against His people with the goal of bringing them to repentance.

What about us? Do we plod along in the familiar or in our own strength? Do we follow wide paths going nowhere or the straight and narrow? God does not want us to be afraid of change or repentance. Sometimes it's best to slow down and turn around. In order to mold and build us into His image, He asks us to seek Him and promises that when we do, we will find Him.

— **KEY VERSE** —

It was because of the LORD's anger that all this happened to Jerusalem and Judah, and in the end he thrust them from his presence. (2 Kings 24:20a, NIV)

GOD TIME

READ : 2 Kings 24:18-25:2
WRITE : 2 Kings 24:20a

REFLECT :
- What truths about God are evident in today's passage?
- This was the third and final invasion of Jerusalem. Look up the years each invasion occurred.
- Add Jehoahaz and Zedekiah (also known as Mattaniah) to the family tree of King Josiah.
- God's judgment is righteous and fierce. Thank God that you are set free from His wrath through Jesus' blood. (Read Romans 5:9 and 1 Thessalonians 5:9)
- Ask God to reveal where you need to be more watchful, slow down, or even turn around.

RESPOND :

PLAN TIME

THINGS TO DO (3-5 MAX) :

KEY EVENTS TODAY :

MOVE TIME

MORNING WATER ☐

B : _____
L : _____
D : _____

SNACK :

SIMPLE WORKOUT ☐

WEEK 1, DAY 3: 2 KINGS 25:8-12, 2 KINGS 17:7 AND 19-20

THERE'S A FAMOUS STORY ABOUT A CHURCH that, in order to develop true worship, did away with the sound system and the band for a while. What was born out of that decision was learning to meet God in a new, heartfelt way. They realized that worship was more than singing. It was about the heart. Out of this experience, Matt Redman's song "The Heart of Worship" was written.

Today we've read about the destruction of Solomon's Temple. Years before, God told David that his son, Solomon (the last king of the united kingdom), would be the one to build His temple. And Solomon did. What a joyous day that must have been for Israel! After years of having a temporary dwelling place for the Ark of the Covenant and a temporary place for the priests to make sacrifices, now Israel had a permanent, holy place of worship.

As Old Testament history went on, though, we know that Israel fell away from God. The second part of today's reading explains how the kings of Judah followed Israel's idolatrous example. They still had the beautiful Temple, altar, silver and gold vessels, menorah, and the Holy of Holies, but they didn't have the right *hearts*. Their worship was halfhearted at best and infiltrated with idolatrous practices. It wasn't about God. It wasn't from the right attitude of the heart.

And so God allowed Nebuchadnezzar to destroy the Temple and city gates and walls during this final siege of Judah (587 BC). Reading about the destruction of the Temple and abuse of God's holy things, leaves me hurt and sad. But God reminds me that it's all about Him, His holiness, and His love. He seeks our true worship. The Israelites wandered so far that they were headed down a dark, horrible path. He allowed them to suffer the consequences, not because He didn't care, but because He cared so much! They were being sanctified. It was being away from Him and away from their homeland that prepared them for their return. It was seeing the destruction of the city and the temple that brought them such great joy when it was all rebuilt.

Rebuilding and renewal are so wonderful. But the events that lead to the need for rebuilding usually aren't. Whether from grief, heartbreak, abuse, straying from God, or whatever else, we need to know that God can rebuild beautifully. (Psalm 23:3) Our concern should be to draw near with worshipful hearts and allow Him to work.

— KEY VERSE —

And he burned the house of the LORD and the king's house and all the houses of Jerusalem; every great house he burned down. (2 Kings 25:9)

Hello mornings
God. Plan. Move.

GOD TIME

READ : 2 Kings 25:8-12, 2 Kings 17:7 and 19-20
WRITE : 2 Kings 25:9

REFLECT :
- Make a list of all the evil things Nebuchadnezzar and his army did in this passage.
- Read Jeremiah 32:4 and 34:3, and Ezekiel 12:13. What was predicted about Zedekiah?
- Read Deuteronomy 28:45-52. This prophecy may have multiple fulfilments and this siege is one.
- Where in your life do you need rebuilding? Thank God for rebuilding and restoring you.
- Draw near to God today in true worship. Pray as He leads.

RESPOND :

PLAN TIME

THINGS TO DO (3-5 MAX) :

KEY EVENTS TODAY :

MOVE TIME

MORNING WATER ☐

B : _____
L : _____
D : _____

SNACK :

SIMPLE WORKOUT ☐

WEEK 1, DAY 4: NEHEMIAH 1:1-3

I PULLED INTO THE CRAMPED GERMAN PARKING GARAGE and squeezed my way into a spot. A colorful sign on the wall before me read "Vorsicht!" I asked my German friend in the car with me to translate. She thought for a split second and replied, "Foresight!" The sign warned me not to pull too far forward. Where we would use the word *caution* (which puts the emphasis on avoiding danger), the German word reminds people to foresee consequences.

Today we've finally started the Book of Nehemiah. We find Nehemiah in the Persian capital city of Susa (which in Hebrew is *Shushan*, which your Bible might say) where we'll later find out he is serving the king. Nebuchadnezzar's Babylonian empire from yesterday's reading has been conquered by the Medo-Persian Empire and the Persian King Artaxerxes is now in power. The year is about 445 BC. Roughly 140 years have passed since the fall of Jerusalem.

And in between, a significant event happened. In the year 539 BC, Cyrus the Great conquered Babylon and in 538 BC made an edict to allow Jews to return home and begin to rebuild the Temple.* Though not all Jews left, 50,000 did and the Temple was completed in 515 BC during Persian King Darius' reign. (This time period is described in Ezra chapters one through six.)

In today's passage, Nehemiah is greeted by his brother Hanani and men from Judah who tell him the conditions of the city of Jerusalem. Nehemiah discovers that his people are in great affliction and that the wall of Jerusalem lay in rubble and the gates remained burned.

Nehemiah knew that his people hadn't followed God. The consequence was discipline. Through idolatry, the Jews had willfully separated themselves from God which resulted in their physical removal from the land and had very real effects on the city of Jerusalem. With broken walls and burned gates, the city had no defense. Jerusalem, once devoted to God, now bore scars of subjugation to foreign kingdoms. The people bore the shame of having no means of restoration. They were a desolate and despised people.

Though incredibly painful, this broken state was a good place to be. As we'll discover, their helplessness opened their hearts to receiving God's restoration. Their story offers hope for the sinner and warns us to think ahead to consequences. It offers a lesson in *vorsicht*!

— **KEY VERSE** —

And they said to me, "The remnant there in the province who had survived the exile is in great trouble and shame. The wall of Jerusalem is broken down, and its gates are destroyed by fire." (Nehemiah 1:3)

*Scholars say the exile began during the first of Nebuchadnezzar's invasions in 605 BC and lasted until the Jews began going home around 538 BC. Allowing for differences in ancient and modern calendars, the exile lasted 70 years.

Hello mornings
God. Plan. Move.

GOD TIME

READ : Nehemiah 1:1-3
WRITE : Nehemiah 1:3

REFLECT :
- Carefully note everything in Hanani's report to Nehemiah.
- Disobedience and rebellion are as old as Adam, Eve, and Cain. What insight does Genesis 4:7 give? What does it mean that Cain could be "accepted?"
- How does Hebrews 12:6, Proverbs 3:12, and Psalm 119:75-76 shed light on God's discipline?
- Have you ever experienced a broken state that became a blessing? What did God do?
- Pray for lost and disobedient loved ones today. Ask God to bring them to repentance.

RESPOND :

PLAN TIME

THINGS TO DO (3-5 MAX) :

KEY EVENTS TODAY :

MOVE TIME

MORNING WATER ☐

B : _____
L : _____
D : _____

SNACK :

SIMPLE WORKOUT ☐

WEEK 1, DAY 5: NEHEMIAH 1:4-11

GOD HAS PLACED MANY GODLY WOMEN IN MY LIFE TO BE MY MENTORS. One particular mentor, Eva, was a woman of dedicated prayer. She's since gone on to be with Lord after living a long, faithful life, but her legacy is not gone. What she modeled to me about going to the Lord in prayer and patiently watching God work is still living. Mentors don't have to be with us to mentor us.

Two things that were really special about Eva was her heart for people and her love for God. When others felt burdened, she felt burdened. She was open and honest in her prayers to God, and didn't fill her prayers with religious talk. Eva had a special relationship with God and ran to her Daddy immediately with her cares and the requests of others. When I prayed with her, I knew her prayers were from a deep place in her heart.

Nehemiah and Eva have some things in common; Nehemiah is also a sort of prayer mentor. After hearing the news about his homeland and people that we discussed yesterday, he went directly to God in prayer. This is the first glimpse we see of Nehemiah's personality and faith. And this first glimpse is a good indicator of the man of faith and prayer that he was.

Not only did Nehemiah go directly to God with a heavy, full heart, He knew God well. I love the list of God's characteristics that he presents in His prayer. When we know God intimately, it's hard to talk to Him without His greatness, lovingkindness, and mercy coming up in the conversation.

Because Nehemiah knew God, he knew His view of sin and understood the judgment God had passed on His people by sending them into exile. Instead of glossing over this as a thing of the past, Nehemiah opens his heart before the Lord and lays out the burden of his nation. When others felt burdened, he felt burdened. Nehemiah fully acknowledged and confessed the sin of Israel. He made no excuses (because he knew there were none anyway) but honestly stated, *"even I and my father's house have sinned. We have acted very corruptly against you…"* (vv. 6b-7a) And after confession, he presented his petition.

If we use Nehemiah's prayer as a model for our own, we see that we can go to God directly, speak to Him intimately, praise His character lovingly, confess to Him wholeheartedly, petition Him reverently, and wait patiently to watch Him work. Mentors don't have to be with us to mentor us!

— **KEY VERSE** —

Let your ear be attentive and your eyes open, to hear the prayer of your servant that I now pray before you day and night. . . (Nehemiah 1:6a)

Hello mornings
God. Plan. Move.

GOD TIME

READ : Nehemiah 1:4-11
WRITE : Nehemiah 1:6a

REFLECT :
- What characteristics of God and mankind does Nehemiah list in his prayer?
- Research the job of the cupbearer. What does this tell us about Nehemiah?
- Read Deuteronomy 30:1-10. This passage is a prophecy of the regathering of Israel and was partially fulfilled by the regathering after captivity. What is the condition in verse two?
- What parts of Nehemiah's prayer stand out to you? Underline them.
- Use Nehemiah's prayer as a model but make it your own. Especially pray verse 11.

RESPOND :

PLAN TIME

THINGS TO DO (3-5 MAX) :

KEY EVENTS TODAY :

MOVE TIME

MORNING WATER ☐

B : _____
L : _____
D : _____

SNACK :

SIMPLE WORKOUT ☐

WEEK TWO
by Karen Bozeman

WEEK 2, DAY 1: NEHEMIAH 2:1-5

SAD HEARTS ARE OFTEN REVEALED IN SAD FACES. How often does your husband or a close friend ask you, "What's wrong?" and you answer "Nothing," but know in your heart this isn't the truth? If you fear spending emotional energy explaining the need only to watch their eyes glaze over, you retreat into your shell.

Nehemiah is faced with a tough situation. He must be completely honest with the king he serves, but he is afraid. We can be encouraged by Nehemiah's action. He doesn't allow fear to rule over him, but instead, seeks God's help immediately.

This man is well-versed in palace protocol. Kings expect people around them to be happy or they are offended. For whatever reason, the heaviness of Nehemiah's heart slips out that day and his face reveals his troubled soul to his employer.

When the king asks him why his face is sad, Nehemiah is *"very much afraid."* He is terrified! Nehemiah stops and prays because he knows only God can determine the response of this powerful king. Nehemiah is about to boldly ask the king for something he is not required to even consider, much less give. He offers a quick prayer, fearful of what might happen next. Artaxerxes can dismiss Nehemiah from the palace or even have him killed.

Refusing to fall into the paralysis of fear, Nehemiah boldly asks the king to send him to Judah. He knows it is not his place to influence the king's heart. This is something only God can do. It is obvious that Nehemiah has an intimate relationship with God because with little time to stop and think, he prays. He has already cultivated a deep relationship with God through hours of prayer. Because of this, he knows God is present in his situation and hears his cry.

When fear overwhelms you because your situation seems impossible, what do you do? Panic? Or pull a Nehemiah and pray? Again, notice that prayer was Nehemiah's instant response to fear. God's response was to give him the courage to make the request to the king. Just as God did for Nehemiah, God will intervene on your behalf.

— **KEY VERSE** —

Then the king said to me, "What are you requesting?" So I prayed to the God of heaven. (Nehemiah 2:4)

GOD TIME

READ : Nehemiah 2:1-5
WRITE : Nehemiah 2:4

REFLECT :
– What lesson did you take away from today's reading? How will you apply it to your life?
– Read Psalm 23. Thank God that He provides even in the presence of enemies.
– In your journal, explore a fear you are facing. Take it to God.
– Write out a prayer asking God to help you with a tough situation.
– Is there a difficult person in your life you'd like to see God change? Pray for them today.

RESPOND :

PLAN TIME

THINGS TO DO (3-5 MAX) :

KEY EVENTS TODAY :

MOVE TIME

MORNING WATER ☐

B : _____
L : _____
D : _____

SNACK :

SIMPLE WORKOUT ☐

WEEK 2, DAY 2: NEHEMIAH 2:6-8

ONE OF THE CORE ROUTINES OF HelloMornings IS PLANNING. It is our goal that the daily plans we make have God's purposes in mind. Nehemiah is a strong example of why "plan" is part of HelloMornings as well as an essential discipline for any growing Christian.

Nehemiah strategically plans what needs to happen for the walls of Jerusalem to be rebuilt. During those months of prayer, Nehemiah isn't formulating his ideas, but God's agenda. When the time is right, Nehemiah is prepared with a ready response.

Back up to verse 5 and capture this conversation. Nehemiah knows King Artaxerxes and how to approach him. Notice he begins in verse 5 by saying, *"If it pleases the king…"* This servant knows that he needs every ounce of tact and grace to address this Persian king. While Nehemiah has position in the court, he doesn't abuse his place. His language is not designed to manipulate Artaxerxes, but to build a bridge so he will listen to the request. He then asks the king to send him to Judah.

King Artaxerxes asks Nehemiah his projected timeline in verse 6: *"How long will you be gone, and when will you return?"* Nehemiah gave him a date of departure. He's already thought this through. Nehemiah not only asks for time away from his job, he asks the king to reverse his decree about repairing the wall and to top it off--pay for repairing it! He's asking for an open purchase order to complete the job.

Why does the king say yes? First, God is with Nehemiah. Nehemiah's prayers are heard and answered. He is asking for God's agenda to be carried out. Second, Nehemiah is a respected servant. I suspect he did his job well, becoming a trustworthy and loyal cupbearer. After all, Artaxerxes wants to know when he's coming back! Because Nehemiah has faithfully served in the court, King Artaxerxes is willing to allow him to go to Judah to complete this project and foot the bill. He built trust with the king and Artaxerxes knows Nehemiah is true to his word.

What does this mean to you and me today? Nehemiah's situation gives us a good model for how to plan: pray, create a plan that is God-honoring, and don't be afraid to ask for help. Remember to give God the credit for the result.

— **KEY VERSE** —

And the king granted me what I asked, for the good hand of my God was upon me. (Nehemiah 2:8b)

GOD TIME

READ : Nehemiah 2:6-8
WRITE : Nehemiah 2:8b

REFLECT :
- Recall a time when the "good hand of God" was upon you. Thank Him for this.
- Do you plan to excess or fail to plan at all? Pray and ask God to help you find balance today.
- What do you need to change in order to have a more productive plan time each day?
- What actions will you take today to seek God's plan for your life? Or to live out His plan?
- Read 2 Corinthians 9:8. Ask God to bless your plans today.

RESPOND :

PLAN TIME

THINGS TO DO (3-5 MAX) :

KEY EVENTS TODAY :

MOVE TIME

MORNING WATER ☐

B : _____
L : _____
D : _____

SNACK :

SIMPLE WORKOUT ☐

WEEK 2, DAY 3: NEHEMIAH 2:9-10

WHEN I DECIDED TO BECOME A FULL-TIME EDUCATOR, I shared my thoughts with my husband. I had my plans laid out. I would quit my job, go back to school to get the needed certification, and then enter the classroom. He was fully supportive of my plan. However, it didn't take long before I was surrounded by opposition. Friends and family were less than enthusiastic about my idea. Other teachers warned me I would fail because it was just too hard. I believed that God was behind me, lovingly guiding me to the place He wanted me to serve Him. I followed His plan.

Nehemiah finds opposition to his God-ordained plan as soon as he arrives at his destination. His feet barely touch the dirt before he is met with disapproval. The governors, Sanballat and Tobiah, are less than thrilled to see Nehemiah appear with letters from the king. Threatened, these two men are angered at Nehemiah's arrival.

You'd think they'd be happy to see him. After all, he's bringing a purchase order to rebuild the wall of Jerusalem. They won't have to lift a finger to help with this project. A fortified city is a good thing. Walls keep out wild animals, thieves, and enemy troops. But these men are opposed to any assistance for the nation Israel.

When we seek to do God's work, hostility and opposition often follow. Satan's agenda is always to make life difficult for us. Guys like Sanballat and Tobiah don't want God back in this city, so they challenge Nehemiah the minute he arrives. Nehemiah's incentive to move forward with this project is the inner knowledge that God is guiding him.

Nehemiah could have retreated. He could have listened to a nagging inner voice that might have said, "This isn't God's will. I am wrong. I'm going to go home." Yet for Nehemiah, this opposition reinforces God's will. Nehemiah has such confidence in God's power and provision that he isn't going to turn back.

How do we get this kind of confidence? The answer can be found in Colossians 2:6-7: *"Therefore, as you received Christ Jesus the Lord, so walk in him, rooted and built up in him and established in the faith, just as you were taught, abounding in thanksgiving."* It's a daily walk, not just when opposition comes. When we are grounded in our faith, we, like Nehemiah, are prepared for the enemy.

— **KEY VERSE** —

But when Sanballat the Horonite and Tobiah the Ammonite servant heard this, it displeased them greatly that someone had come to seek the welfare of the people of Israel. (Nehemiah 2:10)

Hello mornings
God. Plan. Move.

GOD TIME

READ : Nehemiah 2:9-10
WRITE : Nehemiah 2:10

REFLECT :
- The blessing of the king encouraged Nehemiah. Has someone blessed you in your efforts to serve God? Thank that person today.
- Do you have someone who opposes you in your work or ministry? Pray for that person.
- List the who, what, where, when, why, and how of this passage. What do you learn?
- What does today's passage teach you about God and His character?
- Nehemiah traveled 800 miles to do God's work. Does this challenge or encourage you today?

RESPOND :

PLAN TIME

THINGS TO DO (3-5 MAX) :

KEY EVENTS TODAY :

MOVE TIME

MORNING WATER ☐

B : _____
L : _____
D : _____

SNACK :

SIMPLE WORKOUT ☐

WEEK 2, DAY 4: NEHEMIAH 2:11-16

WE HAVE AN UGLY RETAINING WALL that surrounds most of our backyard. It isn't designed for looks, but without it, the backyard and fence would wash into the neighboring woods. When the original wall began to crumble, expert attention was required. My husband had to secure a contractor, negotiate a price, and get a timeline for construction. Replacing the wall required concrete, rebar, and cinder blocks. It was also taking an enormous bite out of our savings, but without this investment, we were going to have a sinkhole in our backyard.

The wall that once surrounded Jerusalem is now a source of shame and disgrace for the returned remnant because it is mostly rubble. A fortified city means safety for those inside. A broken-down wall opens Jerusalem for attacks of wild animals, thieves, and opposing enemies. It is a continual reminder of their defeat. To rebuild the wall would be a sign to the people that God is with them. It would also be a sign to their enemies that they are no longer exposed and open to attack.

Nehemiah inspects the condition of the wall in solitude and silence. He went at night so no one could see him. He's already facing opposition from the governors who don't want a rebuilt Jerusalem. Nehemiah is a hazard to their authority and position because he has the backing of the king. He needs to review the situation without comments from the nay-sayers.

Just as much as we need physical walls, we need personal spiritual walls. Our hearts and minds should be guarded by God and His Word. The enemy is about the business of looking for areas in our lives where we might have a broken-down section in our hearts and minds. This is where he slithers in and takes control.

When was the last time you inspected your wall? Took inventory of your own heart? The stress of the clock presses on all of us - young moms, career women, and caregivers. Before we are aware of the damages, our walls have pieces missing or entire sections that are destroyed.

There is a price for rebuilding a wall, but it is always worth the investment. When we ask God to repair the broken-down places in our lives, Satan is out of a job. Isaiah 30:15b reminds us that *"in quietness and in trust shall be your strength."* Take some quiet moments for inspection.

KEY VERSE

And I told no one what God had put on my heart to do for Jerusalem. (Nehemiah 2:12b)

GOD TIME

READ : Nehemiah 2:11-16
WRITE : Nehemiah 2:12b

REFLECT :
- Are there things in your life that are causing your spiritual walls to crumble? (i.e. social media, Netflix, over-scheduling) What can you eliminate from your life to rebuild your walls?
- Give yourself permission for a "me hour" this week. Do something you enjoy.
- Read Psalm 139. Pray through this psalm and see where your spiritual walls need rebuilding.
- Memorize a verse from Psalm 139 that encourages you.
- What are you doing to help your children build spiritual walls around their hearts and minds?

RESPOND :

PLAN TIME

THINGS TO DO (3-5 MAX) :

KEY EVENTS TODAY :

MOVE TIME

MORNING WATER ☐

B : _____
L : _____
D : _____

SNACK :

SIMPLE WORKOUT ☐

WEEK 2, DAY 5: NEHEMIAH 2:17-20

I HAVE AN AMAZINGLY GIFTED FRIEND NAMED JAN. She can get people to volunteer to help in our church and community ministries. Her influence isn't over a few; she organizes hundreds of people to carry out the tasks that make our Sunday mornings flow smoothly. Jan's teams greet individuals coming on our campus, staff information booths, and make coffee. When she asks for volunteers to help with a special project, people show up by the hundreds. Jan's ability to encourage participation is never about making her look good. It's always about serving God and growing His kingdom.

When Nehemiah appeals for help to rebuild the wall, he doesn't have to beg. He simply tells the people how the hand of God has been favorable to him and how he has received the financial backing of the king. Nehemiah uses the pronoun "us" because he's including himself in the work. The response is "let's do this!" and the people get busy rebuilding the wall.

As we look at Nehemiah's leadership, we can glean three lessons:

1. Godly leaders keep their focus on God alone. If we shift our focus to others, we can become disappointed, disillusioned, and discouraged. We are inviting the nay-sayers to sound off.

2. Godly leaders keep their focus on the ministry they are called to perform. Nehemiah doesn't turn his thoughts to himself. We never hear him express self-pity or concern over personal rejection. He had a God-given vision and sought to fulfill his part in God's plan.

3. Godly leaders know the purpose of God and the people of God are more important than the project. God does His work through people, but His ultimate purpose is to draw people to Himself. Nehemiah presents the plan with enthusiasm and inspires others to join his team of builders. But the end game is not just a wall, but that God will be glorified.

What about you? What is your vision for your life? Is God in the middle of it?

Do you have a plan for your children? Your ministry? Your future? You may be like me. I'm no Jan. I'm not gifted at getting people to join in and rally around a ministry. Yet, it is still God's design to use me for His purposes. I have to be ready to hear Him and roll up my sleeves to do the work.

What steps do you need to take to kick-start a God-given vision?

Then I replied to them, "The God of heaven will make us prosper, and we his servants will arise and build..." (Nehemiah 2:20a)

GOD TIME

READ : Nehemiah 2:17-20
WRITE : Nehemiah 2:20a

REFLECT :
- How are you aware when God desires to speak with you? How does He get your attention?
- Ask yourself, "How am I listening to God today?" What is your response to His voice?
- List specific talents, spiritual gifts, and material possessions God has given you. How might these be used to achieve God's vision for you?
- What actions do you need to take today to seek God's design for your life?
- What big decisions are you thinking about today?

RESPOND :

PLAN TIME

THINGS TO DO (3-5 MAX) :

KEY EVENTS TODAY :

MOVE TIME

MORNING WATER ☐

B : _____
L : _____
D : _____

SNACK :

SIMPLE WORKOUT ☐

WEEK THREE
by Alyssa J Howard

WEEK 3, DAY 1: NEHEMIAH 3:1, 4:1-5

HAVE YOU EVER HIT ROCK BOTTOM? I think we can all agree that at some point in our lives, we messed up. We failed miserably, and we were forced to pick up the pieces to move forward. More often than not, this is easier said than done. What will people say? How will they think of me from here on out? Have I ruined things permanently? Is restoration really possible?

The Jewish people were trying desperately to rebuild, yet they were facing some serious opposition. Sanballat and Tobiah questioned the Jews, hoping they would doubt themselves as well as God. These men mocked the Jews every step of the way. Could the Jews really accomplish all they were trying to rebuild?

If you are anything like me, you have discovered that every time you fail, the enemy is there waiting to kick you while you are down. He is quick to make you feel like there is no coming back from what you have done. If he can convince you that you have no chance of restoration, he can keep you at rock bottom. But this is never God's will for His children. Rebuilding and restoring are His specialties.

It's worth noting that the Jews built the Sheep Gate first. It was by this gate that sacrificial lambs entered the Temple to be slaughtered. By building it first, they demonstrated that reconciliation with God was their main priority. When we fail, where do we begin the rebuilding process? Are we taking the debris of our mistakes to God, or are we opening the gates of our hearts to allow the Lamb of God to wash us clean and make us new?

No matter what, Nehemiah was not going to allow anything to stand in the way of all the Jews were called to accomplish. God wanted them to rebuild both physically and spiritually; and if they were going to be successful, they needed to trust Him and tune out the negative voices. When God calls us to a task, we can rest assured that He will be faithful in giving us the strength we need to do all that He has planned for us. The enemy may try to taunt us. He may even use people in our lives to try to keep us down, but God is good. When we lean on Him for strength and allow Him to renew our hearts, nothing is impossible.

— **KEY VERSE** —

Then Eliashib the high priest rose up with his brothers the priests, and they built the Sheep Gate. They consecrated it and set its doors. (Nehemiah 3:1a)

Hello mornings
God. Plan. Move.

GOD TIME

READ : Nehemiah 3:1, 4:1-5
WRITE : Nehemiah 3:1a

REFLECT :
- Who built the Sheep Gate? What is Jesus referred to in Hebrews 4:14-16?
- In John 10:7-10, who is the Sheep Gate? What will we find when we enter in Him?
- What does it mean that Jesus is our High Priest, the Sheep Gate, and the Lamb who was slain for your sins?
- Can you think of others in Scripture who were mocked for doing the will of God?
- Nehemiah prayed for his enemy's demise. How did Jesus change things in Matthew 5:43-45?

RESPOND :

PLAN TIME

THINGS TO DO (3-5 MAX) :

KEY EVENTS TODAY :

MOVE TIME

MORNING WATER ☐

B : _____
L : _____
D : _____

SNACK :

SIMPLE WORKOUT ☐

WEEK 3, DAY 2: NEHEMIAH 4:6-9

I'M A TO-DO LIST KIND OF GIRL. I set goals, make checklists, and feel accomplished when I get a lot done in one day. But I have to be honest. Some days are better than others. One day I will be working hard to complete the tasks at hand, and the next I will be coming up with every excuse in the book to procrastinate. Fortunately for the Israelites, they had a "mind to work." In spite of opposition, they managed to complete half of their wall.

Half-way through their project, the anger of their enemies was at an all-time high. The Jewish people were actually accomplishing what they set out to do, and their enemies were furious and determined to keep them from progressing any further. I cannot help but notice the spiritual principles in this story. Every time we grow and begin to accomplish something for God, the enemy tries to tear down what we have built. And like the Israelites' physical enemies, our spiritual enemy begins to plot our demise.

Sanballat, Tobiah, and the rest of their enemies came up with a plan to fight Jerusalem and cause confusion. Can you think of a time in your life when the enemy tried to do the very same thing in your own life? 1 Corinthians 14:33 reminds us that confusion does not come from God, rather it is one of the enemy's most used tactics.

Remember Adam and Eve in the Garden of Eden? Satan used confusion and clever deception to trick Eve into believing that eating the fruit was a good choice. His tactics caused her to question God and all He had told her. In the same way, we encounter the enemy's fiery darts and his lies as he tries to confuse us regarding the truth.

There is a lot to be learned spiritually by how the Jewish people responded to their opposition. First of all, they prayed. When it comes to handling the fiery darts of the enemy, prayer is one of our best weapons. Secondly, the Jewish people set a guard as protection. In the same way, we must guard ourselves against the enemy's schemes.

When God calls you to a task, be prepared for the enemy's opposition. But we can also trust that God will give us the tools as well as the strength we need to get the job done.

— **KEY VERSE** —

And we prayed to our God and set a guard as a protection against them day and night. (Nehemiah 4:9)

Hello mornings
God. Plan. Move.

GOD TIME

READ : Nehemiah 4:6-9
WRITE : Nehemiah 4:9

REFLECT :
- Read today's passage again, circling words or phrases that stand out to you.
- Read Ephesians 6:10-18. Which pieces of armor are defensive? Which are offensive?
- According to Ephesians 6:12, who were the real enemies of the God's people as they rebuilt?
- What promise can we cling to in 1 John 5:4-5 as we work to advance God's Kingdom?
- Can you think of a time when the enemy used confusion to keep you from God's plan for your life? How did you respond?

RESPOND :

PLAN TIME

THINGS TO DO (3-5 MAX) :

KEY EVENTS TODAY :

MOVE TIME

MORNING WATER ☐

B : _____
L : _____
D : _____

SNACK :

SIMPLE WORKOUT ☐

WEEK 3, DAY 3: NEHEMIAH 4:10-14

HAVE YOU EVER MADE A DECISION BASED ON FEAR? Whether minor or major, we have all made choices based on our fears. Some of these choices made little impact on our lives, while others changed them forever. I think it is safe to say, however, that fear is never a good motivator in decision-making. We miss God-given opportunities, play it safe when we should be putting our trust in God, and give in to the enemy's schemes by allowing fear into our minds and hearts. And if I have learned anything from fear-based decision-making in my life, it's that it almost always leads to regret.

In today's passage, fear had an opportunity to change things. The men of Judah began to doubt their ability to keep building in the midst of ruins. They looked around at their circumstances and began to feel hopeless. This alone could have been enough to halt their project, but their enemies were not letting up either. Until this point, they had continued to mock and ridicule the Jews, but now these men were threatening to kill the Jews to keep them from building the wall. Even the Jews who lived near the enemy were frightened at what might happen if the building continued.

Yes, fear was definitely the name of the game at this point. What if the Israelites had yielded to this fear? What if they had decided to stop building? As I read this story, it is easy to see that God had His hand in all of this. Although, for Nehemiah, it probably felt like everything was falling apart around him. The people needed a man like him to lead and encourage them to keep up the fight; and in that moment, Nehemiah chose to trust God instead of giving in to his fear.

The Jewish people had a choice to make. They could keep building and fighting for what they knew God had called them to, or they could cower in fear. Sometimes when we face our fears, we have no idea how God is going to intervene. God could have destroyed their enemies in that very moment; but instead, He taught them an important lesson about faith and perseverance.

What is God asking you to entrust to Him? How is He calling you to persevere? When doubt and fear are coming at us from all sides, we can trust that no matter how grim the situation may appear, God is in control and He will accomplish His purposes in our lives.

— **KEY VERSE** —

And I looked and arose and said to the nobles and to the officials and to the rest of the people, "Do not be afraid of them. Remember the Lord, who is great and awesome, and fight for your brothers, your sons, your daughters, your wives, and your homes." (Nehemiah 4:14)

Hello mornings
God. Plan. Move.

GOD TIME

READ : Nehemiah 4:10-14
WRITE : Nehemiah 4:14

REFLECT :
- What does today's passage teach you about handling fear?
- Can you think of a time you allowed fear to influence a major decision? What was the result?
- Read 2 Timothy 1:7 and 1 John 4:18. Where does fear come from and what is the remedy?
- Read Psalm 27. How does this psalm relate to today's passage? How will it encourage you when you face fear or hardships?
- Memorize a verse from Psalm 27 that you can hold onto when facing fear.

RESPOND :

PLAN TIME

THINGS TO DO (3-5 MAX) :

KEY EVENTS TODAY :

MOVE TIME

MORNING WATER ☐

B : _____
L : _____
D : _____

SNACK :

SIMPLE WORKOUT ☐

WEEK 3, DAY 4: NEHEMIAH 4:15-23

IN HIGH SCHOOL, I HAD A FRIEND WHO SUFFERED from a life-long chronic illness. She had good days and bad days. There were some things she could do to help her symptoms, but sometimes she experienced pain for no logical reason. She was on medication and numerous supplements and had to watch her diet. Yet in spite of it all, she was one of the most amazing, God-fearing women I have ever known.

My friend inspired me greatly. When I experienced hard times and difficult battles, she would often come to mind. She was a fighter, but not in the sense that it controlled her life. She experienced all the same joy and laughter as any other high school student. Upon graduating high school, she ventured off to college and is now married with two children. She built a life for herself, all while fighting through her illness.

I cannot help but think of her when reading today's passage. *"…Those who carried burdens were loaded in such a way that each labored on the work with one hand and held his weapon with the other."* (Nehemiah 4:17b) The men of Judah had a job to get done, and they were determined to finish it. Can you imagine trying to build a wall while holding a weapon? Not only would it be logistically difficult, but also rather frightening. At any moment, their enemies could attack.

We have all had to fight at some point in our lives. We fight for our marriages, our kids, our careers, our friendships, and sometimes even our faith. Fighting is simply a part of life. But as Christians, we are also called to build. Every day, we are working together to advance the Kingdom.

I love the image of building with one hand while holding a weapon in the other. It is a beautiful picture of the Christian life. We are building the Kingdom with one hand and holding the sword of the Spirit in the other. But there is one key difference between Nehemiah's imagery and what is true for us as Christians. The sword of the Spirit is the most powerful weapon of all time. Unlike the Jewish people, we can build with no fear. If attacked by the enemy, we know our victory is secure.

— **KEY VERSE** —

Those who carried burdens were loaded in such a way that each labored on the work with one hand and held his weapon with the other. (Nehemiah 4:17b)

Hello mornings
God. Plan. Move.

GOD TIME

READ : Nehemiah 4:15-23
WRITE : Nehemiah 4:17b

REFLECT :
- Read today's passage again. Circle any words or phrases that stand out to you.
- What do we learn about God's sovereignty and faithfulness in Nehemiah 4:15?
- What do we learn about our spiritual weapons in 2 Corinthians 10:3-5?
- Journal about a time in your life when you had to simultaneously build and fight. How did God help you through that time?
- What are you currently fighting for in your life? Take that fight to God in prayer.

RESPOND :

PLAN TIME

THINGS TO DO (3-5 MAX) :

KEY EVENTS TODAY :

MOVE TIME

MORNING WATER ☐

B : _____
L : _____
D : _____

SNACK :

SIMPLE WORKOUT ☐

WEEK 3, DAY 5: NEHEMIAH 5:1, 6-11

"BUT IT'S NOT FAIR!" MY THREE-YEAR-OLD DAUGHTER WAS CRYING. Her older sister had set up an imaginary play home in our living room and refused to allow her younger sibling to enter. "You need three tickets to enter, and you don't have any tickets!" By this point, my youngest daughter's cries had turned into sobs. I knew it was time to intervene.

If there is one thing I've learned in my short time as a parent, it is that justice plays a key role. Not only does the Bible tell us that true love is just, but it is also one of the attributes of our heavenly Father. The Old Testament Law is filled with examples of God's justice. Many of the laws dealt with ownership and a person's rights when something was taken from them. God cared about these small details, so as a parent, I know I should strive to do the same.

In today's passage, Nehemiah needed to intervene. He heard the cries of those who were being mistreated. The wealthy were taking advantage of the poor in their need to borrow money. It was a mess, to say the least. There are two things to note in this story. First of all, the people felt free to take their complaints to Nehemiah. He was obviously a leader who was willing to listen. Secondly, Nehemiah did something about it. He stood for justice even if it meant coming against wealthy and influential men.

When my daughters fight or mistreat one another, I try to see it as an opportunity to show them how God's justice works. Often when we think of His justice, we think of punishment, but truth be told, justice is far more than that. When my youngest tries to get her older sister to do her chores, I intervene. When a toy is taken, I return it to its rightful owner. The Jewish people were being mistreated and taken advantage of, and Nehemiah executed justice by fighting on their behalf.

How often do we as Christians step in to help those less fortunate? Do we stand in the gaps and fight for justice? By taxing the poor, the nobles and officials were giving their enemies ammunition to mock them and put down God. The same is true today. When we mistreat people, we give them reason to doubt the God we serve. Let us never forget that everything we do is a reflection of God's Kingdom and its King.

— KEY VERSE —

So I said, "The thing that you are doing is not good. Ought you not to walk in the fear of our God to prevent the taunts of the nations our enemies?" (Nehemiah 5:9)

Hello mornings
God. Plan. Move.

GOD TIME

READ : Nehemiah 5:1, 6-11
WRITE : Nehemiah 5:9

REFLECT :
- What did Nehemiah do in verse 7 before addressing the complaints of the people?
- Read Ezekiel 16:49. What was Sodom's greatest sin and how does this affect your view of God's justice?
- Read 1 John 3:16-18. What does this passage teach about God's heart for those in need?
- Memorize 1 John 3:18.
- Ask God to bring someone to mind who needs you. Pray for an opportunity to help.

RESPOND :

PLAN TIME

THINGS TO DO (3-5 MAX) :

KEY EVENTS TODAY :

MOVE TIME

MORNING WATER ☐

B : _____
L : _____
D : _____

SNACK :

SIMPLE WORKOUT ☐

WEEK FOUR
by Ayoka Billions

WEEK 4, DAY 1: NEHEMIAH 6:1-9

I HAVE HAD THE PLEASURE OF LOVING ALMOST EVERY JOB that I have ever had-from my first job waiting tables for Ryan's Steak House at the age of 16 to writing test questions last year from home. Except that "one." It was not just bad; it was miserable. It produced chest-pain inducing stress levels. The difficulties came not because of the leadership or the clients, but because I had several enemies working alongside me. They tried to decrease my productivity by sending me on wild goose chases and refusing to lend a hand. But things got really bad when they tried to fill my heart with fear. Receiving a phone call on Christmas Eve from my boss about a potentially life-threatening situation—that turned out to be a lie—truly scared me. Having someone mockingly ask, "You're scared, aren't you?" made a lump stick in my throat that didn't go away. I would love to say that I stayed and fought, but their tactics worked. I turned in my resignation letter and stopped working for that company out of fear of these enemies. Their actions, coupled with my very natural reactions, ended what could have been a great job for me, and I walked away.

Sanballat, Tobiah, Geshem, and the rest of Nehemiah's enemies were just as ruthless, but he had his eyes on the prize. He knew that his job was too important to be stopped. The tactics were fierce: distraction and fear. As human beings, we are naturally susceptible to both of these. Distraction strikes as we are pressing forward towards the prize, and then the air conditioner dies and the water heater leaks. Or we receive news of a tough medical diagnosis or family crisis leading to major conflict. These are normal life distractions, but Nehemiah's enemies were even more sinister; they planned to harm him as he turned aside. I absolutely love Nehemiah's response in verse 3: *"I am doing a great work and I cannot come down."* His discernment and faithfulness probably saved his life.

When distraction did not work, the enemies turned to lies that would induce fear in the heart of Nehemiah. Nehemiah's response was two-fold. First, he rebutted the lie by speaking truth. Next, he prayed to God for strength. Nehemiah wasn't super-human. He was obviously nervous after these encounters, but he did not let it stop him from his work.

— **KEY VERSE** —

I am doing a great work and I cannot come down. (Nehemiah 6:3)

Hello mornings
God. Plan. Move.

GOD TIME

READ : Nehemiah 6:1-9
WRITE : Nehemiah 6:3

REFLECT :
- Read 1 Corinthians 9:24-27. How did Nehemiah live out this passage?
- What prize are you pressing towards during this season of your life?
- Write down three ways that the enemy has tried to distract you.
- What is one way that you have been able to overcome fear in your life?
- Write out the following statement and say it out loud a few times: "I am doing a great work and I cannot come down.?

RESPOND :

PLAN TIME

THINGS TO DO (3-5 MAX) :

KEY EVENTS TODAY :

MOVE TIME

MORNING WATER ☐

B : _____
L : _____
D : _____

SNACK :

SIMPLE WORKOUT ☐

WEEK 4, DAY 2: NEHEMIAH 6:10-14

AS A YOUNG AND INEXPERIENCED DRIVER, I was zipping along a two-lane country road while fumbling with my car stereo on a slightly wet day. The next thing that I knew, I was hydroplaning and completely lost control of the vehicle. I breathed a prayer as I prepared to meet my maker. After unbuckling and crawling out, I realized that I was miraculously unharmed. A few scrapes from broken glass were my only injuries that day. My guardian angels had been faithful.

Later that afternoon, emergency department staff confirmed the assessment by the paramedics at the scene: no physical injuries. But they could not measure the fear that had been unleashed in my life. I was terrified to get behind the wheel of a car again. My wise father gave me one week to recover—physically, mentally, and emotionally—and then told me that if I wanted to go anywhere, I would have to drive myself to get there. He knew that my fears, though very natural, had become harmful to my emotional well-being. My fears were impacting the actions of my life and, if left unchecked, could destroy me. The fear had turned to action.

Nehemiah's enemies knew the power of fear. They knew that if fear is allowed to stay unchecked, it turns into negative actions. And they used this knowledge to their advantage. In his case, they were attempting to scare him into acting in a manner that contradicted the Lord's commands to his people. Their own tactics had not worked, so they hired someone very influential to attack with words to inspire fear. *"They are coming to kill you by night"* (v. 10) was the report that Nehemiah heard that day. What could be worse than hearing those words from a pillar in the community? According to the local prophet, a spiritual leader, these enemies were going to come under cover of darkness, perhaps while Nehemiah was sound asleep, and take his life. Once again, the wise Nehemiah recognized the trap set for him and went to the Lord in prayer to turn the situation over to God.

Likewise, the enemy of our souls understands the negative power of fear. In the New Testament, we read many accounts of God's people being tempted by fear. And over and over, God offers us the reassuring command: Do not fear.

— **KEY VERSE** —

For this purpose he was hired, that I should be afraid and act in this way and sin. (Nehemiah 6:13a)

Hello mornings
God. Plan. Move.

GOD TIME

READ : Nehemiah 6:10-14
WRITE : Nehemiah 6:13a

REFLECT :
- What was the prophet attempting to get Nehemiah to do?
- Had he listened, Nehemiah would have left his people without a leader. What could have happened?
- Read Ps. 118:5-7. How does God protect us during fearful situations?
- Journal: During the past week, in what ways have I acted out of fear?
- List people who have done you wrong. Ask for His forgiveness to move through you today.

RESPOND :

PLAN TIME

THINGS TO DO (3-5 MAX) :

KEY EVENTS TODAY :

MOVE TIME

MORNING WATER ☐

B : _____
L : _____
D : _____

SNACK :

SIMPLE WORKOUT ☐

WEEK 4, DAY 3: NEHEMIAH 6:15-19

WHEN I LIVED IN LOS ANGELES, I worked in a large hospital that saw its fair share of celebrities. Even though we regularly saw well-known entertainment and political figures, reports of celebrity sightings still sent ripples throughout the facility. One day, I had my own experience: a famous actor opened a door for me as I moved through the halls. I happily offered a "Thank you" before realizing who he was. He replied with a pleasant "You're welcome" and we both continued about the day. As I continued on, I couldn't help but be excited at this little exchange and I still remember it today.

I think that people are somehow wired to give honor to those that we feel are important: people with important positions, power, money, or fame or related to those who are. Unfortunately for Nehemiah, his biggest enemy, Tobiah, was related to not one—but two—important people which caused the nobles of Judah to be duty-bound to offer their support to Tobiah.

After Nehemiah had coordinated the completion of the wall in only 52 days, all the nations around were afraid because they recognized that the Israelites had only succeeded through help from their God. But some of God's own people were unable (or unwilling) to recognize the hand of the Lord in Nehemiah's work. Verse 19 states that *"Tobiah sent letters to make me afraid."*

One has to wonder if they were blinded to seeing the obvious hand of God in the rebuilding project because of who Tobiah was. Is it possible to completely miss the will of God by following a person? Have I ever missed God's will in this manner?

Tobiah's followers remind me of another group of men who followed a leader, only this time, they were following God's anointed one: the soon-to-be King David. May I be like David's men! These faithful servants followed God's will despite being hunted by King Saul, the most powerful man in the land. (see I Samuel 23-34). Perhaps they had heard about that dinner where David was anointed by Samuel to be the next king. We will probably never know this side of heaven (P.S. I am adding these men to my mental list of folks to chat with when I get to heaven), but the important part is how they followed without wavering and were not discouraged by being on the wrong side of earthly power.)

— **KEY VERSE** —

And when all our enemies heard of it, all the nations around us were afraid and fell greatly in their own esteem, for they perceived that this work had been accomplished with the help of our God. (Nehemiah 6:16)

Hello mornings
God. Plan. Move.

GOD TIME

READ : Nehemiah 6:15-19
WRITE : Nehemiah 6:16

REFLECT :
- Read 1 Samuel 22:6-10. Why did Doeg tell Saul what Abimelech had done for David?
- Ask yourself: Have I ever been willing to stand up against a powerful person?
- Yesterday, we made a list of people who have done us wrong. Take a few minutes to pray for someone on that list.
- What can you do this week to bless someone on that list?
- Write our Proverbs 25:6-7. What does this passage say about dealing with important people?

RESPOND :

PLAN TIME

THINGS TO DO (3-5 MAX) :

KEY EVENTS TODAY :

MOVE TIME

MORNING WATER ☐

B : _____
L : _____
D : _____

SNACK :

SIMPLE WORKOUT ☐

WEEK 4, DAY 4: NEHEMIAH 7:1-4

WHILE WORKING AS A NURSING SUPERVISOR, I was tasked with finding someone to promote to a leadership position. Without their knowing, I watched men and women carry out daily tasks in my search for someone capable of carrying out a leadership role.

Why? Groups of people need strong leaders. Leaders have helped to inspire me to pursue Jesus, go to college, go back to college, grow as a person, share my faith with others, and pursue excellence in everyday life. Strong leaders look for strong leaders. Nehemiah has already proven his faithfulness and dedication as a true servant-leader. Now, he was looking for someone to place in charge of the entire city of Jerusalem.

So, what was he looking for? A lot. First, he was looking for faithfulness to the work at hand. Who had been willing to sacrifice to see the wall rebuilt? Who had continued when the going got tough? Who had been unwilling to give in to whining and complaints during this grueling project?

Next, he was looking for a man who feared God. In modern English, this phrase can be very confusing. Nehemiah wasn't looking for men who were scared of God. Proverbs 1:7 tells us that *"The fear of the Lord is the beginning of knowledge."* Writer and speaker John Bevere puts it this way: "When we fear God, we choose to love what He loves and hate what He hates." He goes on to say that "fear of God" boils down to one simple thing: obedience.

People who fear God:
- Obey Him instantly.
- Obey Him even if it doesn't make sense.
- Obey Him even if it hurts.
- Obey Him even if they don't see the benefit.
- Obey Him to completion.

Nehemiah chose his brother, Hanani, who displayed these traits of faithfulness and obedience. Verse 2 tells us that *"he was a more faithful and God-fearing man than many."* He and Hananiah were given charge over Jerusalem and instructions to keep the residents safe. They were told when to open and close the gates and instructed to choose guards from among the people of Jerusalem. And we see the leader selection process continue once more.

— **KEY VERSE** —

I gave my brother Hanani and Hananiah the governor of the castle charge over Jerusalem, for he was a more faithful and God-fearing man than many. (Nehemiah 7:2)

Hello mornings
God. Plan. Move.

GOD TIME

READ : Nehemiah 7:1-4
WRITE : Nehemiah 7:2

REFLECT :
- Read Luke 16:10. What does Jesus say about showing yourself to be faithful?
- Why is it hard for children to obey at times?
- Have you ever found it hard to obey what God was directing you to do?
- Write out Proverbs 1:7. What do we learn about foolish people?
- What little thing is God asking you to be faithful in today? Write it down and share it with someone for accountability.

RESPOND :

PLAN TIME

THINGS TO DO (3-5 MAX) :

KEY EVENTS TODAY :

MOVE TIME

MORNING WATER ☐

B : _____
L : _____
D : _____

SNACK :

SIMPLE WORKOUT ☐

WEEK 4, DAY 5: NEHEMIAH 7:5-7, 66, 73

AS A GIRL GROWING UP IN THE SOUTH, I was often asked "Who are your people?" Older folks always wanted to know who my parents and grandparents were, mostly out of curiosity to find out if they knew my descendants. They wanted to have knowledge of my genealogy. I would quickly give an account of my grandparents, aunts, uncles, and cousins. The names, approximate ages, and home communities of my family members were of great interest during these encounters since prior generations placed a greater importance upon knowing one's personal history than we do today. It was often fun to hear their memories of my family from their school days. I recently had an opportunity to hear new school-time stories from my mother. These stories gave me a better understanding of who my mother was as a young girl and what helped shape who she is today. But even more so, it helps me to know who I am.

Nehemiah wanted to know exactly which families had been taken into exile. He recognized that those people and their descendants had a shared history that had seen ups and down and needed to be remembered. More than anything, Nehemiah wanted to bring these families home to a city that could now be kept safe. Their homecoming was the ultimate completion of a project that had consumed his focus for months. God gave Nehemiah the idea to review the history of the Jewish nation and organize the return of the people by tribes and families.

Why is our history important? In order to understand our purpose, we must understand who we are. As Christ-followers, we are able to trace our roots back only one generation: to God, our Father. We spend time each morning seeking His face to know who He is. Once we have confessed and believed, we can be sure that our name is written in the greatest genealogy book of all: the Book of Life. Our salvation story helps us to know who we are and where we belong.

— **KEY VERSE** —

Then my God put it into my heart to assemble the nobles and the officials and the people to be enrolled by genealogy. (Nehemiah 7:5a)

Hello mornings
God. Plan. Move.

GOD TIME

READ : Nehemiah 7:5-7, 66, 73
WRITE : Nehemiah 7:5a

REFLECT :
- Write out Matthew 1:1. Which three names are mentioned in this verse? Why?
- Why do you think God directed the Gospel writers to begin with this verse?
- Read Matthew 1:17. How many generations back can you trace on your family tree?
- Do you remember when you became a Christ-follower?
- Take a few minutes to write down your story as a follower of Jesus. Who can you share it with this week?

RESPOND :

PLAN TIME

THINGS TO DO (3-5 MAX) :

KEY EVENTS TODAY :

MOVE TIME

MORNING WATER ☐

B : _____
L : _____
D : _____

SNACK :

SIMPLE WORKOUT ☐

WEEK FIVE
by Jennifer McLucas

WEEK 5, DAY 1: NEHEMIAH 8:1-12

SOMETIMES I OPEN MY BIBLE and I start to read and nothing happens. I read it, I understand the meaning of the words, but I miss the point. I don't see how the scripture relates to my real life. I miss the message.

The Israelites were excited as they gathered. They came together as a large congregation to listen to Ezra read the Scriptures. I'm sure they greeted each other happily in the cool of the morning, but as the sun rose higher, the air got warmer. Stale. Sticky. Yet still they stood attentive, ears and hearts wide open, straining to hear every word spoken. They stood, silent, for as long as six hours. They were listening intently, letting the words sink in.

As Ezra read, the Levites explained. It was important that the whole assembly understood what was being read. The Israelites needed to understand the message. They needed to see how it connected to their lives now.

As the Law was read, the Israelites were moved to tears. Their hearts were tender and open and they understood how they had missed the mark. They felt the weight of their sins and they were grieved.

Like the Israelites, when we read God's Word and really understand the weight of what it says, we should be moved. 2 Timothy 3:16 says, *"All Scripture is breathed out by God and profitable for teaching, for reproof, for correction, and for training in righteousness..."* When we read scripture, we should expect something to happen inside us. We should expect a reaction as God's Word penetrates our hardened hearts.

If we want to grow as Christians, we must read the Bible with the intent that it will change us. We must look for the ways in which we need to change. We need to, in prayer, ask the right questions. What is God teaching me through this passage? Does this passage indicate that I am doing something God doesn't approve of? Is there something I need to change? What have I read that I need to apply to my life or way of thinking?

The Israelites, on this day, were asking the right questions. Let us follow their example.

— KEY VERSE —

They read from the book, from the Law of God, clearly, and they gave the sense, so that the people understood the reading. (Nehemiah 8:8)

Hello mornings
God. Plan. Move.

GOD TIME

READ : Nehemiah 8:1-12
WRITE : Nehemiah 8:8

REFLECT :
- Read Nehemiah 8:9. Explain in your own words why the people wept.
- What does Matthew Henry's commentary say about why the people wept? (You can find this commentary online at biblestudytools.com)
- Have you ever been grieved by your sin? What verses helped you find your joy in the Lord?
- Who can you share these verses with today?
- What does today's study lead you to pray?

RESPOND :

PLAN TIME

THINGS TO DO (3-5 MAX) :

KEY EVENTS TODAY :

MOVE TIME

MORNING WATER ☐

B : _____
L : _____
D : _____

SNACK :

SIMPLE WORKOUT ☐

WEEK 5, DAY 2: NEHEMIAH 8:13-18

MY FAVORITE TIME OF DAY IS MY TWO MONTH OLD DAUGHTER'S BATHTIME. Not because it's particularly fun for me, but because she enjoys it so much. It brings a smile to my face to watch her happily splash and kick her legs. She smiles and coos at the washcloth as I wipe away the soap. She's happy in the bath and it makes me happy to make her happy.

There is great joy in doing as the Lord asks of us, of knowing we are doing what is right in the eyes of our Lord. That's because we know that He delights in us when we follow His commands and we want Him to be pleased with us. It's one of our most basic desires. C.S. Lewis calls this "the joy of the inferior" in his sermon, *The Weight of Glory*. He explains the joyous result of pleasing God saying,

"…When the redeemed soul, beyond all hope and nearly beyond belief, learns at last that she has pleased Him whom she was created to please. There will be no room for vanity then. She will be free from the miserable illusion that it is her doing. With no taint of what we should now call self-approval she will most innocently rejoice in the thing that God has made her to be…"

The Israelites were grateful that God was faithfully fulfilling His promises to them. They were saddened that they had been disobedient for so long. The Israelites longed to please the God who had been so faithful to them. As Ezra was reading the Law, their hearts were open to hearing it. They wanted to know how they could please God. They were eager to put into practice what they read.

Matthew Henry says, *"Those that diligently search the scriptures will find those things written there which they had forgotten or not duly considered,"* and *"We read and hear the word acceptably and profitably when we do according to what is written therein, when what appears to be our duty is revived after it has been neglected."*

God's commands are meant to be so much more than just a list of rules. Great joy can be found in pleasing God by doing as He has called us to do.

— **KEY VERSE** —

And all the assembly of those who had returned from the captivity made booths and lived in the booths, for from the days of Jeshua the son of Nun to that day the people of Israel had not done so. And there was very great rejoicing. (Nehemiah 8:17)

Hello mornings
God. Plan. Move.

GOD TIME

READ : Nehemiah 8:13-18
WRITE : Nehemiah 8:17

REFLECT :
- Read today's passage again. Describe the scene in your own words.
- Research the Feast of the Tabernacles. Write down what you learn.
- How is the Feast of the Tabernacles relevant to you today?
- Read Psalm 118:25. In what areas of your life do you need God to answer this prayer for you today?
- List seven people you can "invite" into what you are learning through this study.

RESPOND :

PLAN TIME

THINGS TO DO (3-5 MAX) :

KEY EVENTS TODAY :

MOVE TIME

MORNING WATER ☐

B : _____
L : _____
D : _____

SNACK :

SIMPLE WORKOUT ☐

WEEK 5, DAY 3: NEHEMIAH 9:1-5

I DON'T KNOW ABOUT YOU, but when I get ready for church I put on my best clothes, my Sunday best if you will. Even though jeans with holes and activewear are very common for my day-to-day style, I would never wear either to church. Dressing for church isn't just vanity. I've been brought up to see it as a sign of respect.

The Israelites did not wear their best in today's passage, instead they wore old rags and poured dirt on their heads. They dressed for mourning. We read in chapter 8 earlier this week that the Israelites were instructed not to mourn their sin. This was because it was the Feast of Trumpets, a holy day of celebration and not an appropriate time to mourn. Today, we're coming full circle. On this day, the Israelites came together for the very purpose of mourning their sin.

I love what Matthew Henry has to say regarding this change in behavior, *"The joy of our holy feasts must give way to the sorrow of our solemn fasts when they come. Everything is beautiful in its season."*

This day was to be a day of mourning and repentance for the Israelites. Back in chapter 8 they started weeping because they heard the Law read to them and understood the depths of their sin, but on this day they went a step further. On this day they met together and, after reading the Law for several hours, they made a public confession of all their sins. They dressed for mourning because it was a serious and sorrowful affair. It was also beautiful.

I love that the Israelites had become so desperate for God in their lives. They had remembered all that He had done for them. They believed that He had the power to provide them with a good future. They had hope. They had faith. They wanted a deeper relationship.

This is why the Word of God is so important. It proves powerful in our lives over and over again. God uses His Word in our lives to show us the things that we need to confess. Sometimes it hurts a little, but it always leads us into deeper relationship with Him. It's always worth the discomfort. God's Word, including the Law, is always intended to bring us into deeper relationship with Him.

— **KEY VERSE** —

Now on the twenty-fourth day of this month the people of Israel were assembled with fasting and in sackcloth, and with earth on their heads. (Nehemiah 9:1)

Hello mornings
God. Plan. Move.

GOD TIME

READ : Nehemiah 9:1-5
WRITE : Nehemiah 9:1

REFLECT :
- Read the passage again. Sketch the scene.
- What does Matthew Henry's commentary say reading the Law will do for us? (You can find this commentary online at biblestudytools.com)
- When was the last time Scripture called you to an act of obedience to the Lord?
- Does today's passage lead you to confess anything?
- What do you need to pray?

RESPOND :

PLAN TIME

THINGS TO DO (3-5 MAX) :

KEY EVENTS TODAY :

MOVE TIME

MORNING WATER ☐

B : _____
L : _____
D : _____

SNACK :

SIMPLE WORKOUT ☐

WEEK 5, DAY 4: NEHEMIAH 9:6-8, 22-23, 26, 30-31

I SAT IN MY CAR JUST STARING INTO SPACE. I was overwhelmed. I was a freshman in college, feeling scared and alone. I was in an abusive relationship. I knew I needed to get out, but I didn't know how. I didn't know who to talk to. I didn't know who I could trust for help. At times I felt like I deserved the abuse, certain it was my fault. I worried things would get worse instead of better. I was afraid to move. I wondered where God was in all of this mess. I questioned whether or not He would help me.

Today we are given a great history lesson. Today we go all the way back to the creation. We see God's provision for us from the very beginning. We see how God called Abram and fulfilled all His promises to him. We see how the Israelites rebelled, despite God's great care of them. We see the Israelites acknowledge they deserved the discipline they were receiving and they profess that it is only because of God's great mercy that they are still alive.

One of the best ways to find the courage to move forward is to look at the past. When we look to the past, we are reminded that it was God who created everything. From the dawn of time He has been providing for us. It was God who called us to follow Him. It was God who gave us hope for a future. It was God who has faithfully fulfilled all His promises to us. Even when we get ourselves into a mess of our own making, it is God who sets us free.

God is merciful. He wants to save us. He wants us to trust in His faithfulness.

Sitting in my car that night, I called out to God and He answered me. He showed me the way out. He moved me to where I needed to be. Remembering God's faithfulness in the past should always move us to trust Him with our present. God is always moving through our story, even in the most difficult parts of life. God does not forsake us, rather, in His great mercy, He redeems every situation.

— **KEY VERSE** —

Nevertheless, in your great mercies you did not make an end of them or forsake them, for you are a gracious and merciful God. (Nehemiah 9:31)

Hello mornings
God. Plan. Move.

GOD TIME

READ : Nehemiah 9:6-8, 22-23, 26, 30-31
WRITE : Nehemiah 9:31

REFLECT :
- Read today's passage again, outlining the brief history given.
- Read Judges 2:6-3:6 which expounds on today's reading. What do you note?
- Is there an area of your own life in which you feel stuck in the same kind of pattern? Pray for God's deliverance.
- Journal about a time when God has been faithful in your past.
- Thank God for his faithfulness.

RESPOND :

PLAN TIME

THINGS TO DO (3-5 MAX) :

KEY EVENTS TODAY :

MOVE TIME

MORNING WATER ☐

B : _____
L : _____
D : _____

SNACK :

SIMPLE WORKOUT ☐

WEEK 5, DAY 5: NEHEMIAH 9:32-37

WHEN MY DAD WAS DIAGNOSED WITH TERMINAL BRAIN CANCER in January of 1998, my internal world changed. Drastically. I longed to really have the faith that others seemed to see in me, but there were moments when I doubted. Lots of them. I didn't know how to handle the doubt. I wondered if I was really a Christian. Christians aren't supposed to doubt.

In today's passage, the Israelites cry out to God. They beg for His mercy, asking that He would see the suffering they have experienced as sufficient. They acknowledge God's faithfulness. They admit their wickedness. They understand their suffering is necessary for their correction.

Sometimes our actions make us feel far away from God. Other times our circumstances make us feel far away from God. But God keeps His covenant with us. He keeps His promise to walk with us, close beside us.

Sometimes pain and sorrow are necessary for our improvement. We need to trust Him in the pain. He knows what we need and He knows what we can bear. There is no sorrow we suffer that seems small to Him. And He won't let our pain be wasted. Rather, He will use our suffering to draw us deeper into relationship with Him.

God is always drawing us closer to Himself. It is the one certainty we can always depend on. However much we may know our own weaknesses and doubt our own sincerity of faith, we can always depend on His love and faithfulness. God always keeps His covenant. God's love is truly steadfast. Whatever circumstances we may face, God's commitment to us remains unchanged. We can't escape it and our doubt doesn't erase it.

I have come to the opinion that there is no little hardship. Life is hard. Doubt comes fast. Too fast. The only way to combat doubt is with Truth, capital "T" Truth. However big our hardship is, however big our doubt, God can be trusted. He sees us. He knows us. He has a plan for us. The best thing we can do is call out to Him in faith. Even if it's just a tiny bit of faith.

— **KEY VERSE** —

Now, therefore, our God, the great, the mighty, and the awesome God, who keeps covenant and steadfast love, let not all the hardship seem little to you that has come upon us, upon our kings, our princes, our priests, our prophets, our fathers, and all your people, since the time of the kings of Assyria until this day. (Nehemiah 9:32)

Hello mornings
God. Plan. Move.

GOD TIME

READ : Nehemiah 9:32-37
WRITE : Nehemiah 9:32

REFLECT :
– Read today's passage again. What promises or warnings do you see?
– Read Romans 8:18-30. What similarities do you see?
– Reflect on your past. How has God used hardship for your good?
– Who can you share these thoughts with today?
– What does today's study lead you to pray?

RESPOND :

PLAN TIME

THINGS TO DO (3-5 MAX) :

KEY EVENTS TODAY :

MOVE TIME

MORNING WATER ☐

B : _____
L : _____
D : _____

SNACK :

SIMPLE WORKOUT ☐

WEEK SIX
by Kelli LaFram

WEEK 6, DAY 1: NEHEMIAH 12:27-30, 40-43

HOSTING CHRISTMAS AND THANKSGIVING DINNERS used to be the most stressful and joyless thing for me. I would gladly volunteer to have family over, but by the time the planning, the cleaning, cooking, and the hosting were finished, I was finished. Done. Worn out. Anything but joyful.

In today's passage, I see a whole lot of work being done in order to have a party. Okay, not exactly a party, but a big event nonetheless. It was the dedication of the wall of Jerusalem. And it took quite a lot of work. Sending people out to gather the Levites. Others traveling many, many miles while packing along musical instruments. Priests purifying themselves, purifying the people, and purifying the gate. Plus an organization of two marching bands (see verses 31-39).

All of this was done, just so they could then sing and praise and worship. This was followed by an offering of sacrifices (again, not an easy task). I'm exhausted just imagining all the prep work that they had to do. And they did it all without modern-day conveniences.

But do you know what really amazes me? They did it all with joy. Not just any joy, but God-given joy. *"For God had made them rejoice with great joy."* (v. 43) Why is it that God gives some people joy and not others? Why didn't He give me joy when I was hosting big holiday dinners?

Why? Because of thankfulness. Verse 27 tells us that the Israelites came to Jerusalem *"to celebrate the dedication with gladness, both with **thanksgiving** and singing..."* They were given joy because they were thankful for all that God had done for them. He had brought them back from a foreign land and restored them to their home. He had restored their place of worship. He had rebuilt their city walls. He had kept His promises to them. Not because they deserved it, but because He said He would. Oh, what a trustworthy God! And dwelling on all this led God's people to thankfulness which produced a joyfulness that only God could get the credit for.

Yes, hosting holiday dinners and organizing city wall dedications can be a lot of work, but if we focus on the work instead of the reason for the celebration we will miss out on joy every time. As children of God we have much to be thankful for. When we choose to keep our focus on Jesus, we can trust God to produce joy in us … even when there is a ton of the work to be done.

— **KEY VERSE** —

And they offered great sacrifices that day and rejoiced, for God had made them rejoice with great joy; the women and children also rejoiced. And the joy of Jerusalem was heard far away. (Nehemiah 12:43)

Hello mornings
God. Plan. Move.

GOD TIME

READ : Nehemiah 12:27-30, 40-43
WRITE : Nehemiah 12:43

REFLECT :
- Verse 43 says that the "joy of Jerusalem was heard far away." Can your joy be seen or heard from far away? Why or why not?
- When you have a mountain of work to do, how can you trust God in the situation?
- Read Psalm 35:9 and 51:7-12, and Isaiah 12:1-3. What should we base our joy on?
- In a Christian's life, how are trust and joy related? Share your thoughts with a friend.
- What has this passage taught you about God?

RESPOND :

PLAN TIME

THINGS TO DO (3-5 MAX) :

KEY EVENTS TODAY :

MOVE TIME

MORNING WATER ☐

B : _____
L : _____
D : _____

SNACK :

SIMPLE WORKOUT ☐

WEEK 6, DAY 2: NEHEMIAH 12:44-47

DO YOU REMEMBER WHEN YOU FIRST dedicated or rededicated your life to the Lord? It was awesome, right? For most of us, we experienced some sort of excitement. We were on a spiritual high. Our adrenaline was pumping and it felt good to do all that we could for God's kingdom.

This is most likely the same type of experience the Israelites were going through in today's passage. They'd just celebrated the dedication of the wall, they'd been assigned their duties, and they were serving and giving with gladness. God had done much for them and their thanksgiving had produced a God-given joy and their joy had turned to action. For the time being. they were keeping the requirements of the Law. However, as we will see in the rest of the book of Nehemiah, it did not last. They would soon choose worldly pleasure over God's Word.

Spiritual highs feel good and we want to stay on them; though the experiences are natural and good, they don't last. The truth of the matter is, as children of God, we will experience highs, middles, and lows as we walk with the Lord. How we react to the mundane-middles and the not-so-thrilling lows is just as important as how we react to the highs.

The Bible says, *"The Lord is good to those who wait for him, to the soul who seeks him."* (Lamentations 3:25) The psalmists declared, *"I wait for the Lord, my soul waits, and in his word I hope,"* (Psalm 130:5) and *"I would have lost heart, unless I had believed that I would see the goodness of the Lord in the land of the living."* (Psalm 27:13, NKJV)

When our spiritual highs end, we must continue to seek the Lord, wait on the Lord, and believe in the Lord. Otherwise we will go off looking for something that feels good, just as the Israelites did.

A spiritual high feels good, but so does sin. If we are honest about our personal choices, we understand why it was so easy for the Israelites to turn from God. They wanted, as we often do, to experience something that felt good. Let's learn from their mistakes. Let's choose to trust in what God says is good, not what makes us feel good.

— **KEY VERSE** —

I wait for the Lord, my soul waits, and in his word I hope...(Psalm 130:5)

Hello mornings
God. Plan. Move.

GOD TIME

READ : Nehemiah 12:44-47
WRITE : Psalm 130:5

REFLECT :
- Are you experiencing a spiritual high, middle, or low today? How can you trust God in it?
- Read Psalm 1 and 1 John 2:15-17. How do they relate to today's passage?
- Consider your own thoughts and behaviors. When is it easiest to serve God? Is easy always better?
- Write down any questions you may have. You can answer them later.
- Do you feel led to confess anything? Do so in prayer.

RESPOND :

PLAN TIME

THINGS TO DO (3-5 MAX) :

KEY EVENTS TODAY :

MOVE TIME

MORNING WATER ☐

B : _____
L : _____
D : _____

SNACK :

SIMPLE WORKOUT ☐

WEEK 6, DAY 3: NEHEMIAH 13:1-14

HAVE YOU HEARD THE TERM "UNEQUALLY YOKED?" It's when a child of God enters into a close relationship with a nonbeliever. These relationships, if not saturated in prayer, often have a far greater effect on the believer than on the nonbeliever. We should not isolate ourselves from nonbelievers; however, we need to follow God's counsel when deciding who we have intimate friendships with.

Between the end of Nehemiah 12 and the beginning of chapter 13, there was a 10-12 year gap in which Nehemiah had spent time away from Jerusalem. When he returned, he found that the revival of Israel had faded drastically, many Israelites had married pagans and Eliashib the priest had been befriended by Tobiah the Ammonite (remember, the man who had plotted and schemed against Nehemiah back in chapter six).

Why is this a big deal? Because God had forbid it. The Israelites were not to allow any Moabite or Ammonite into their assembly. Not because of the color of their skin or their nationality, but because of their desire to curse Israel. (see Genesis 12:3) The Moabites and Ammonites were pagan; however, if one were to turn his or her back on their idols and choose to serve the one true God, God would see him or her as an Israelite (Numbers 15:14-16). Ruth, for example, was a Moabite who chose the God of Israel (Ruth 1:16) and God blessed her for her decision.

Tobiah was not an Ammonite who chose God as Ruth did. Neither were many of the foreign people the Israelites had married. The Bible doesn't tell us exactly what Eliashib or the others were thinking. Maybe it was, "This really isn't a big deal—I can handle it," or "I really love this person—God will understand."

He understands that good friends will encourage us to do right, while wicked ones will only help us go astray. 2 Corinthians 6:14 says, *"Do not be unequally yoked with unbelievers. For what partnership has righteousness with lawlessness? Or what fellowship has light with darkness?"*

When we choose to ignore what God says about our relationships, what does our behavior say? It says we trust ourselves more than we trust God. It says, "God doesn't really know me. He doesn't understand what I can handle. I can't and I don't trust God with this decision."

However, when we choose to give our decisions and relationships over to God, and obey His word, then we truly exhibit trust in Him.

— **KEY VERSE** —

Do not be unequally yoked with unbelievers. For what partnership has righteousness with lawlessness? Or what fellowship has light with darkness? (2 Corinthians 6:14)

Hello mornings
God. Plan. Move.

GOD TIME

READ : Nehemiah 13:1-14
WRITE : 2 Corinthians 6:14

REFLECT :
– Learn more about the Balaam incident. Read Numbers 22-25.
– Consider why relationships matter. Read Proverbs 12:26 and 2 Corinthians 6:14-18.
– Do you have any close relationships with nonbelievers? How do these people influence you?
– What do you trust more: God's Word or your ability to handle unequally yoked relationships?
– Are you married to an unbeliever? Read 1 Corinthians 7:13-14 and this article:
  https://www.thegospelcoalition.org/article/honoring-god-in-an-unequally-yoked-marriage

RESPOND :

PLAN TIME

THINGS TO DO (3-5 MAX) :

KEY EVENTS TODAY :

MOVE TIME

MORNING WATER ☐

B : _____
L : _____
D : _____

SNACK :

SIMPLE WORKOUT ☐

WEEK 6, DAY 4: NEHEMIAH 13:15-22

EVERY ONCE IN AWHILE I'LL BE IN THE MIDDLE of doing one chore or another and my husband will call to me, as I rush by him, "Come have a seat." "No, Hun," I'll say, "I've really got to get another (fill in the blank) done." He's so sweet, I'll think to myself, but by the third or fourth time that he has asked me to sit with him, I'm flat out annoyed. *Doesn't he realize all the work I need to get done?*

I don't know exactly why the Israelites refused to keep the Sabbath. I don't know the exact excuses they made to justify their disobedience to God, but I'm sure it had something to do with trust. They didn't trust that God knew what was best for them. They didn't trust that when He said, "You need rest," that they really needed rest.

I hate to tell you this, but we're a lot like the Israelites. Like them, we need rest. And like them, we often refuse to take it. I'm not suggesting we should attempt to keep the Sabbath. We are no longer under the Law, we are under grace (see James 2:10 and Romans 6:14). However, we have been invited to rest.

Jesus says, *"Come to me, all who labor and are heavy laden, and I will give you rest."* (Matthew 11:28) And do you know what? I think He means it. He will actually give us rest—physical, emotional, mental, and spiritual—if we only come to Him. Spend time with Him. Take pleasure in Him.

If we take a minute to ponder, we might realize that the reason we don't rest is we don't trust God either. We may trust that a spotless house or a perfectly prepared meal will give us true pleasure. We may trust that a happy boss/client/spouse will make us happy. We may trust and believe that one day we will get to the end of our to-do list and we will experience calm delight. But these things never quite bring us joy, do they?

I may not trust that my husband's call to come rest is always best. My heavenly Father, though, gives a call to rest I can always trust. I want to listen and obey because I know that He loves me more than any other and that what He is calling me to do is always good.

— **KEY VERSE** —

Come to me, all who labor and are heavy laden, and I will give you rest. (Matthew 11:28)

Hello mornings
God. Plan. Move.

GOD TIME

READ : Nehemiah 13:15-22
WRITE : Matthew 11:28

REFLECT :
- Read about the Sabbath: Exodus 20:8-11, Matthew 11:28-30, Mark 2:27, and Hebrews 4:9.
- The word *burden* appears in Nehemiah 13:15 and Matthew 11:30. Define and compare the original Hebrew and Greek words.
- Read Isaiah 58:13-14. What did God promise to Israel if they would honor the Sabbath?
- Does the promise from Isaiah 58:13-14 apply to us today? How so?
- Talk to God and listen to how He wants you find rest.

RESPOND :

PLAN TIME

THINGS TO DO (3-5 MAX) :

KEY EVENTS TODAY :

MOVE TIME

MORNING WATER ☐

B : _____
L : _____
D : _____

SNACK :

SIMPLE WORKOUT ☐

WEEK 6, DAY 5: NEHEMIAH 13:23-31

HAVE YOU EVER MADE A PROMISE TO GOD? Have you ever sworn up and down that you would never do a, b, or c again? Or maybe you promised that you would do x, y, or z forever? How did it go? Were you able to keep your word? Or did you break your oath over and over and over again?

Earlier in the book of Nehemiah, Ezra had read God's Word, the people confessed their sins and they took an oath to walk in God's Law and do all that He commanded. It sounds like the perfect formula for a righteous life—read, confess, promise, walk—but there is a small flaw. Actually, it's a big flaw and I fear that most of us, myself included, haven't realized the problem.

The flaw? The oath. The promise. The *reliance* on *self* to do all that God commands. You see here in chapter 13 evidence that mankind cannot *keep* his promises to God. No matter how much we want to, we are not able to keep God's holy standard. The Israelites couldn't do it, and even though Nehemiah *made them* take the oath again (v. 25), they were destined to fail over and over.

When we make promises to God to keep His Word we may have good intentions, but we are trusting in ourselves, the creation, rather than the Creator. We can't *keep*, we can't do, we can't follow the way we were initially designed to—even though we may really, really want to. Not on our own anyway. We must be completely and desperately dependent on God's grace, the work of the cross, and the Holy Spirit to keep us from doing anything that is wicked. He *keeps*. We can't.

David put it this way, *"The Lord will **perfect** that which concerns me...."* (Psalm 138:8, NKJV) The Lord does the perfecting, the sanctifying, and the cleansing of unrighteousness. Not us. I'll be honest, where God's responsibility ends and mine begins is confusing to me. But I do know this for sure: we must have faith—we must trust the Lord and Him alone to keep and perfect us.

— KEY VERSE —

The Lord will perfect that which concerns me... (Psalm 138:8, NKJV)

Hello mornings
God. Plan. Move.

GOD TIME

READ : Nehemiah 13:23-31
WRITE : Psalm 138:8

REFLECT :
- Read Psalm 138:8 and 141:3-10. Who does the psalmist depend on for sanctification?
- Have you noticed the theme of trust in this week's commentary? What does it mean to trust God?
- Read Matthew 5:33-37 and James 5:12. What do these verses tell us about taking oaths?
- Consider what this passage teaches us about mankind. Do you need to confess anything?
- Write 3-5 truths, commands, or promises that you have learned from the Book of Nehemiah.

RESPOND :

PLAN TIME

THINGS TO DO (3-5 MAX) :

KEY EVENTS TODAY :

MOVE TIME

MORNING WATER ☐

B : _____
L : _____
D : _____

SNACK :

SIMPLE WORKOUT ☐

CONCLUSION

I TRULY PRAY THAT YOU ENJOYED WALKING THROUGH THE BOOK OF NEHEMIAH and that this study has blessed you!

We covered quite a bit of Old Testament history and even looked at some difficult topics. But there's one thing we touched on over and over again. God is good! He is the God of renewal. He rebuilds and He restores! No matter where we are in our walk with Him, He has work to do on us. And it's good work, indeed. We must draw near in faithful obedience and allow our loving, merciful God to perform His wonderful works of renewal.

I pray that you'll close the pages of this study reminded of God's power. No task is too great for Him and no care of ours is too small. He repairs our brokenness and restores our souls!

In Him,

Ali

ABOUT THE AUTHORS

ALI SHAW can't believe how blessed life is! As a Central Texas wife, momma, and new grandma, Ali leads a full, grace-filled life. She serves as the HelloMornings Bible Study Director and owns and writes for *DoNotDepart.com* and is generally in awe that God will use a regular girl like her! Woven with practical insight, her writing encourages women to seek God daily through the reading and study of His Word. Most of her writing can be found through HelloMornings or DoNotDepart, but she blogs occasionally at her personal blog, *HeartfeltReflections.wordpress.com* where she's written an online Bible study, Learning from Job. She has also authored an in depth Bible study of Abigail. For information or encouragement, you can connect with her on Facebook at *www.facebook.com/heartfeltreflectionsblog*.

ALYSSA J. HOWARD is a wife and stay-at-home mom to two young girls, and she is thrilled to be a part of her third HelloMornings Bible study. She lives with her family in the Pacific Northwest where she loves to bake, run, drink coffee, and play with her little ones. Alyssa first fell in love with writing while earning her Master of Arts degree in theological studies from Liberty Theological Seminary, and she has been blogging about Jesus and the Christian life for the past three years at *www.alyssajhoward.com*. You can also find her on Facebook at *www.facebook.com/lyssjhoward*.

AYOKA BILLIONS is a wife, mother of 3 boys, business-owner, and very part-time nurse. She enjoys reading, writing, organizing, and inspires others through instruction that connects to the heart. In her spare time, she loves to work in her vegetable garden, go for hikes, and sit outside with a cup of hot coffee and a book. Ayoka joined HelloMornings several years ago and now serves as the Leadership Manager.

JENNIFER MCLUCAS lives outside Portland, Oregon with her insightful husband, her three lovely daughters, and her three wild sons. Jennifer is a writer, speaker, and ministry leader devoted to encouraging women through this messy-beautiful life. Jennifer truly believes that everyone has a calling and writes to inspire others to live out that calling. Jennifer endeavors to teach women to look for God in life's everyday moments through her writing and speaking. She shares encouragement from her faith, stories about her crazy-good life, and occasional book reviews on her website *jennifermclucas.com*. She has coauthored several Bible studies including *New Beginnings*, *But We See Jesus parts 1 & 2*, and *A Life On Purpose* for Hello Mornings. She is also a regular contributor for the Portland Mom's Blog and writer for Western Seminary. Jennifer would love to connect on Facebook and Instagram.

KAREN BOZEMAN is a wife and empty-nester. Her adult children moved far from their East Texas roots, so she travels often. A public-school teacher for 20 years, Karen is now an on-line college English instructor. It is her joy to write and edit projects for her church and various ministries. Karen has been a leader for HelloMornings for over a year and serves as the Ministry Coordinator for the thriving Connect Group that her husband teaches in their local church. In addition, Karen leads women's studies in her home and at church. She and her husband have been married for nearly 40 years. You can follow her Twitter at *twitter.com/kbozeman*.

KELLI LAFRAM is a wife, mom, coffee-drinker, Bible-reader, and a Jesus believer; plus a writer, painter, & sign-maker. She has authored And *When You Pray: Understanding the Lord's Prayer* available at *gumroad.com/l/WpNZ* and Caught by *Jesus: a 6-Week Study in the Gospel of Mark* available on Amazon. You can find her at www.KelliLaFram.com sharing all that she can to point you to God's goodness, His grace, and His glory.

Made in United States
North Haven, CT
25 August 2023